The Great Duke of Florence by Philip Massinger

Philip Massinger was baptized at St. Thomas's in Salisbury on November 24th, 1583.

Massinger is described in his matriculation entry at St. Alban Hall, Oxford (1602), as the son of a gentleman. His father, who had also been educated there, was a member of parliament, and attached to the household of Henry Herbert, 2nd Earl of Pembroke. The Earl was later seen as a potential patron for Massinger.

He left Oxford in 1606 without a degree. His father had died in 1603, and accounts suggest that Massinger was left with no financial support this, together with rumours that he had converted to Catholicism, meant the next stage of his career needed to provide an income.

Massinger went to London to make his living as a dramatist, but he is only recorded as author some fifteen years later, when The Virgin Martyr (1621) is given as the work of Massinger and Thomas Dekker.

During those early years as a playwright he wrote for the Elizabethan stage entrepreneur, Philip Henslowe. It was a difficult existence. Poverty was always close and there was constant pleading for advance payments on forthcoming works merely to survive.

After Henslowe died in 1616 Massinger and John Fletcher began to write primarily for the King's Men and Massinger would write regularly for them until his death.

The tone of the dedications in later plays suggests evidence of his continued poverty. In the preface of The Maid of Honour (1632) he wrote, addressing Sir Francis Foljambe and Sir Thomas Bland: "I had not to this time subsisted, but that I was supported by your frequent courtesies and favours."

The prologue to The Guardian (1633) refers to two unsuccessful plays and two years of silence, when the author feared he had lost popular favour although, from the little evidence that survives, it also seems he had involved some of his plays with political characters which would have cast shadows upon England's alliances.

Philip Massinger died suddenly at his house near the Globe Theatre on March 17th, 1640. He was buried the next day in the churchyard of St. Saviour's, Southwark, on March 18th, 1640. In the entry in the parish register he is described as a "stranger," which, however, implies nothing more than that he belonged to another parish.

Index of Contents

INTRODUCTION

This play, under the title of The Great Duke, was licensed by Sir Henry Herbert, July 5th, 1627. The plot is raised on those slight materials afforded by our old chroniclers in the life of Edgar, which Mason has since worked up into the beautiful drama of Elfrida.

The first edition of this play was published 1636, when it was preceded by two commendatory copies of verses by G. Donne and J. Ford. Though highly and most deservedly popular, it was not reprinted. This may be attributed, in some measure, to the growing discontent of the times, which perversely turned aside from scenes like these, to dwell with fearful anxiety on those of turbulence and blood.—It is impossible not to be charmed with the manner in which this play is written. The style is worthy of the most polished stage. An easy elevation and a mild dignity are preserved throughout, which afford an excellent model for the transaction of dramatic business between persons of high rank and refined education. As to the subject, it is of itself of no great importance; but this is somewhat compensated by the interest the principal characters take in it, and the connexion of love with the views of state.—The scenes between Giovanni and Lidia present a most beautiful picture of artless attachment, and of that unreserved innocence and tender simplicity which Massinger describes in so eminently happy a manner. Were it not for the scene of low buffoonery in the fourth act, where Petronella assumes the dress and character of her mistress, The Great Duke of Florence would have been a perfect and unrivalled production.

TO THE TRULY HONOURED, AND MY NOBLE FAVOURER, SIR ROBERT WISEMAN, KNT.[1] OF THORRELL'S HALL, IN ESSEX.

SIR,

As I dare not be ungrateful for the many benefits you have heretofore conferred upon me, so I have just reason to fear that my attempting this way to make satisfaction (in some measure) for so due a debt, will further engage me. However, examples encourage me. The most able in my poor quality have made use of dedications in this nature, to make the world take notice (as far as in them lay) who and what they were that gave supportment and protection to their studies; being more willing to publish the doer, than receive a benefit in a corner. For myself, I will freely, and with a zealous thankfulness, acknowledge, that for many years I had but faintly subsisted, if I had not often tasted of your bounty. But it is above my strength and faculties to celebrate to the desert your noble inclination, and that made actual, to raise up, or, to speak more properly, to rebuild the ruins of demolished poesie. But that is a work reserved, and will be, no doubt, undertaken, and finished, by one that can to the life express it. Accept, I beseech you, the tender of my service; and in the list of those you have obliged to you, contemn not the name of

Your true and faithful honourer,
PHILIP MASSINGER.

FOOTNOTE:

[1] Sir Robert Wiseman was the eldest son of Richard Wiseman, a merchant of London, who, having acquired an ample fortune, retired into Essex, in which county he possessed considerable estates, where he died in 1618, and was succeeded by Sir Robert. The friend of Massinger was the oldest of fourteen children, and a man of an amiable character. He died unmarried the 11th May, 1641, in his sixty-fifth year.—GILCHRIST.

DRAMATIS PERSONÆ

COZIMO, Duke of Florence.
GIOVANNI, nephew to the duke.
SANAZARRO, the duke's favourite.
CAROLO CHAROMONTE, GIOVANNI's tutor.
CONTARINO, secretary to the duke.
ALPHONSO,   }
HIPPOLITO,   } counsellors of state.
HIERONIMO,   }
CALANDRINO, a merry fellow, servant to GIOVANNI.
BERNARDO,   }
CAPONI,   } servants to CHAROMONTE.
PETRUCHIO,   }
A Gentleman.

FIORINDA, Duchess of Urbin.
LIDIA, daughter to CHAROMONTE.
CALAMINTA, servant to FIORINDA.
PETRONELLA, a foolish servant to LIDIA.

Attendants, Servants, &c.

THE GREAT DUKE OF FLORENCE

ACT I

SCENE I

The Country. A Room in Charomonte's House.

Enter **CHAROMONTE** and **CONTARINO**.

CHAROMONTE
You bring your welcome with you.

CONTARINO
Sir, I find it
In every circumstance.

CHAROMONTE
Again most welcome.
Yet, give me leave to wish (and pray you excuse me,
For I must use the freedom I was born with)
The great duke's pleasure had commanded you
To my poor house upon some other service;
Not this you are design'd to: but his will
Must be obey'd, howe'er it ravish from me
The happy conversation of one
As dear to me as the old Romans held
Their household Lars, whom they believed had power
To bless and guard their families.

CONTARINO
'Tis received so
On my part, signior; nor can the duke
But promise to himself as much as may
Be hoped for from a nephew. And 'twere weakness
In any man to doubt, that Giovanni[1],
Train'd up by your experience and care
In all those arts peculiar and proper
To future greatness, of necessity
Must in his actions, being grown a man,
Make good the princely education
Which he derived from you.

CHAROMONTE
I have discharged,
To the utmost of my power, the trust the duke
Committed to me, and with joy perceive
The seed of my endeavours was not sown
Upon the barren sands, but fruitful glebe,
Which yields a large increase: my noble charge,
By his sharp wit, and pregnant apprehension,
Instructing those that teach him; making use,
Not in a vulgar and pedantic form,
Of what's read to him, but 'tis straight digested,
And truly made his own. His grave discourse,
In one no more indebted unto years,
Amazes such as hear him: horsemanship,
And skill to use his weapon, are by practice
Familiar to him: as for knowledge in
Music, he needs it not, it being born with him;
All that he speaks being with such grace deliver'd,
That it makes perfect harmony.

CONTARINO
You describe
A wonder to me.

CHAROMONTE
Sir, he is no less;
And that there may be nothing wanting that
May render him complete, the sweetness of
His disposition so wins on all
Appointed to attend him, that they are
Rivals, even in the coarsest office, who
Shall get precedency to do him service;
Which they esteem a greater happiness
Than if they had been fashion'd and built up
To hold command o'er others.

CONTARINO
And what place
Does he now bless with his presence?

CHAROMONTE
He is now
Running at the ring[2], at which he's excellent.
He does allot for every exercise
A several hour; for sloth, the nurse of vices,
And rust of action, is a stranger to him.
But I fear I am tedious; let us pass,

If you please, to some other subject, though I cannot
Deliver him as he deserves.

CONTARINO
You have given him
A noble character.

CHAROMONTE
And how, I pray you,
(For we, that never look beyond our villas,
Must be inquisitive,) are state affairs
Carried in court?

CONTARINO
There's little alteration:
Some rise, and others fall, as it stands with
The pleasure of the duke, their great disposer.

CHAROMONTE
Does Lodovico Sanazarro hold
Weight and grace with him?

CONTARINO
Every day new honours
Are shower'd upon him, and without the envy
Of such as are good men; since all confess
The service done our master in his wars
'Gainst Pisa and Sienna may with justice
Claim what's conferr'd upon him.

CHAROMONTE
'Tis said nobly;
For princes never more make known their wisdom,
Than when they cherish goodness where they find it:
They being men, and not gods, Contarino,
They can give wealth and titles, but no virtues;
That is without their power. When they advance,
Not out of judgment, but deceiving fancy,
An undeserving man, howe'er set off
With all the trim of greatness, state, and power,
And of a creature even grown terrible
To him from whom he took his giant form,
This thing is still a comet, no true star;
And when the bounties feeding his false fire
Begin to fail, will of itself go out,
And what was dreadful proves ridiculous.
But in our Sanazarro 'tis not so,
He being pure and tried gold; and any stamp

Of grace, to make him current to the world,
The duke is pleased to give him, will add honour
To the great bestower; for he, though allow'd
Companion to his master, still preserves
His majesty in full lustre.

CONTARINO
He, indeed,
At no part does take from it, but becomes
A partner of his cares, and eases him,
With willing shoulders, of a burden which
He should alone sustain.

CHAROMONTE
Is he yet married?

CONTARINO
No, signior, still a bachelor; howe'er
It is apparent that the choicest virgin
For beauty, bravery, and wealth, in Florence,
Would, with her parents' glad consent, be won,
Were his affection and intent but known
To be at his devotion.

CHAROMONTE
So I think too.
But break we off—here comes my princely charge.

[Enter **GIOVANNI** and **CALANDRINO**.

Make your approaches boldly; you will find
A courteous entertainment.

[**CONTARINO** kneels.

GIOVANNI
Pray you, forbear
My hand, good signior; 'tis a ceremony
Not due to me. 'Tis fit we should embrace
With mutual arms.

CONTARINO
It is a favour, sir,
I grieve to be denied.

GIOVANNI
You shall o'ercome:
But 'tis your pleasure, not my pride, that grants it.

Nay, pray you, guardian, and good sir, put on:
How ill it shows to have that reverend head
Uncover'd to a boy!

CHAROMONTE
Your excellence
Must give me liberty to observe the distance
And duty that I owe you.

GIOVANNI
Owe me duty!
I do profess (and when I do deny it,
Good fortune leave me!) you have been to me
A second father, and may justly challenge,
For training up my youth in arts and arms,
As much respect and service as was due
To him that gave me life. And did you know, sir,
Or will believe from me, how many sleeps
Good Charomonte hath broken, in his care
To build me up a man, you must confess
Chiron, the tutor to the great Achilles,
Compared with him, deserves not to be named.
And if my gracious uncle, the great duke,
Still holds me worthy his consideration,
Or finds in me aught worthy to be loved,
That little rivulet flow'd from this spring;
And so from me report him.

CONTARINO
Fame already
Hath fill'd his highness' ears with the true story
Of what you are, and how much better'd by him;
And 'tis his purpose to reward the travail
Of this grave sir with a magnificent hand:
For though his tenderness hardly could consent
To have you one hour absent from his sight,
For full three years he did deny himself
The pleasure he took in you, that you, here,
From this great master, might arrive unto
The theory of those high mysteries
Which you, by action, must make plain in court.
'Tis, therefore, his request, (and that, from him,
Your excellence must grant a strict command,)
That instantly (it being not five hours' riding)
You should take horse and visit him. These his letters
Will yield you further reasons.

[Delivers a packet.

CALANDRINO
To the court!
Farewell the flower, then, of the country's garland.
This is our sun, and when he's set we must not
Expect or spring or summer, but resolve
For a perpetual winter.

CHAROMONTE
Pray you, observe

[**GIOVANNI** reading the letters.

The frequent changes in his face.

CONTARINO
As if
His much unwillingness to leave your house
Contended with his duty.

CHAROMONTE
Now he appears
Collected and resolved.

GIOVANNI
It is the duke!
The duke, upon whose favour all my hopes
And fortunes do depend; nor must I check
At his commands for any private motives
That do invite my stay here, though they are
Almost not to be master'd. My obedience,
In my departing suddenly, shall confirm
I am his highness' creature; yet I hope
A little stay to take a solemn farewell
Of all those ravishing pleasures I have tasted
In this my sweet retirement, from my guardian
And his incomparable daughter, cannot meet
An ill construction.

CONTARINO
I will answer that:
Use your own will.

GIOVANNI
I would speak to you, sir,
In such a phrase as might express the thanks
My heart would gladly pay; but—

CHAROMONTE
I conceive you:
And something I would say; but I must do it
In that dumb rhetoric which you make use of;
For I do wish you all—I know not how,
My toughness melts, and, spite of my discretion,
I must turn woman.

[Embraces **GIOVANNI**.

CONTARINO
What a sympathy
There is between them!

CALANDRINO
Were I on the rack,
I could not shed a tear. But I am mad,
And, ten to one, shall hang myself for sorrow
Before I shift my shirt. But hear you, sir,
(I'll separate you), when you are gone, what will
Become of me?

GIOVANNI
Why, thou shalt to court with me.

[Takes **CHARAMONTE** aside.

CALANDRINO
To see you worried?

CONTARINO
Worried, Calandrino!

CALANDRINO
Yes, sir: for, bring this sweet face to the court,
There will be such a longing 'mong the madams,
Who shall engross it first, nay, fight and scratch for 't,
That, if they be not stopp'd—So much for him.
There's something else that troubles me.

CONTARINO
What's that?

CALANDRINO
Why, how to behave myself in court, and tightly.
I have been told the very place transforms men,
And that not one of a thousand, that before
Lived honestly in the country on plain salads,

But bring him thither, mark me that, and feed him
But a month or two with custards and court cake-bread,
And he turns knave immediately.—I'd be honest;
But I must follow the fashion, or die a beggar.

GIOVANNI
And, if I ever reach my hopes, believe it,
We will share fortunes.

CHAROMONTE
This acknowledgment

lEnter **LIDIA**.

Binds me your debtor ever.—Here comes one
In whose sad looks you easily may read
What her heart suffers, in that she is forced
To take her last leave of you.

CONTARINO
As I live,
A beauty without parallel!

LIDIA
Must you go, then,
So suddenly?

GIOVANNI
There's no evasion, Lidia,
To gain the least delay, though I would buy it
At any rate. Greatness, with private men
Esteem'd a blessing, is to me a curse;
And we, whom, for our high births, they conclude
The only freemen, are the only slaves.
Happy the golden mean! Had I been born
In a poor sordid cottage, not nursed up
With expectation to command a court,
I might, like such of your condition, sweetest,
Have ta'en a safe and middle course, and not,
As I am now, against my choice, compell'd
Or to lie groveling on the earth, or raised
So high upon the pinnacles of state,
That I must either keep my height with danger,
Or fall with certain ruin.

LIDIA
Your own goodness
Will be your faithful guard.

GIOVANNI
O, Lidia!—

CONTARINO [Aside.
So passionate[3]!

GIOVANNI
For, had I been your equal,
I might have seen and liked with mine own eyes,
And not, as now, with others'; I might still,
And without observation or envy,
As I have done, continued my delights
With you, that are alone, in my esteem,
The abstract of society: we might walk
In solitary groves, or in choice gardens;
From the variety of curious flowers
Contemplate nature's workmanship and wonders:
And then, for change, near to the murmur of
Some bubbling fountain, I might hear you sing,
And, from the well-tuned accents of your tongue,
In my imagination conceive
With what melodious harmony a quire
Of angels sing above their Maker's praises:
And then with chaste discourse, as we return'd,
Imp[4] feathers to the broken wings of time:—
And all this I must part from.

CONTARINO
You forget
The haste imposed upon us.

GIOVANNI
One word more,
And then I come. And after this, when, with
Continued innocence of love and service,
I had grown ripe for hymeneal joys,
Embracing you, but with a lawful flame,
I might have been your husband.

LIDIA
Sir, I was,
And ever am, your servant; but it was,
And 'tis, far from me in a thought to cherish
Such saucy hopes. If I had been the heir
Of all the globes and sceptres mankind bows to,
At my best you had deserved me; as I am,
Howe'er unworthy, in my virgin zeal

I wish you, as a partner of your bed,
A princess equal to you; such a one
That may make it the study of her life,
With all the obedience of a wife, to please you.
May you have happy issue, and I live
To be their humblest handmaid!

GIOVANNI
I am dumb,
And can make no reply.

CONTARINO
Your excellence
Will be benighted.

GIOVANNI
This kiss, bathed in tears,
May learn you what I should say.

LIDIA
Give me leave
To wait on you to your horse.

CHAROMONTE
And me to bring you
To the one half of your journey.

GIOVANNI
Your love puts
Your age to too much trouble.

CHAROMONTE
I grow young,
When most I serve you.

CONTARINO
Sir, the duke shall thank you.

[Exeunt.

FOOTNOTES

[1] *Giovanni.*] *This word is used as a quadrisyllable. This is incorrect, and shows that Massinger had studied the language in books only: no Italian would or could pronounce it in this manner. He makes the same mistake in the name of the duchess:—Fiorinda is a trisyllable; yet he adopts the division of poor Calandrino, and constantly pronounces it Fi-o-rin-da.—GIFFORD.*

[2] Running at the ring.] This amusement made a part of nearly all those magnificent spectacles which used to be given on public occasions. A ring of a very small diameter was suspended by a string from a kind of gibbet, of which the horizontal beam moved on a swivel. At this the competitors ran with their spears couched, with loose reins, and, as the public regulations have it, "as much speed as the horses have." The object was to carry off the ring on the point of the spear, which was light, taper, and adapted to the purpose. It was of difficult attainment; for, from an account of a match made by King Edward the Sixth, seventeen against seventeen, of which he has left a description, it appears, that "in one hundred and twenty courses the ring was carried off but three times."—King Edward's Journal, p. 26. The victor was usually rewarded with a ring set with precious stones, and bestowed by the lady of the day.

[3] So passionate!] i. e. so deeply affected. In this sense the word perpetually occurs in our old writers.

[4] To imp.] i. e. to insert a new feather into the wing of a hawk in the place of a broken one.—These lines are perhaps the most beautiful of a scene eminently graceful and elegant.

SCENE II

Florence. A Room in the Palace.

Enter **ALPHONSO, HIPPOLITO,** and **HIERONIMO.**

ALPHONSO
His highness cannot take it ill.

HIPPOLITO
However,
We with our duties shall express our care
For the safety of his dukedom.

HIERONIMO
And our loves

[Enter **COZIMO.**

To his person.—Here he comes: present it boldly.

[They kneel: **ALPHONSO** tenders a paper.

COZIMO
What needs this form? We are not grown so proud
As to disdain familiar conference
With such as are to counsel and direct us.
This kind of adoration show'd not well
In the old Roman emperors, who, forgetting
That they were flesh and blood, would be styled gods:
In us to suffer it were worse. Pray you, rise.

[Reads.

Still the old suit! With too much curiousness
You have too often search'd this wound, which yields
Security and rest, not trouble, to me.
For here you grieve that my firm resolution
Continues me a widower; and that
My want of issue to succeed me in
My government, when I am dead, may breed
Distraction in the state, and make the name
And family of the Medici, now admired,
Contemptible.

HIPPOLITO
And with strong reasons, sir.

ALPHONSO
For were you old, and past hope to beget
The model of yourself, we should be silent.

HIERONIMO
But being in your height and pride of years,
As you are now, great sir; and having, too,
In your possession the daughter of
The deceased Duke of Urbin, and his heir,
Whose guardian you are made; were you but pleased
To think her worthy of you, besides children,
The dukedom she brings with her for a dower
Will yield a large increase of strength and power
To those fair territories which already
Acknowledge you their absolute lord.

COZIMO
You press us
With solid arguments, we grant; and, though
We stand not bound to yield account to any
Why we do this or that, (the full consent
Of our subjects being included in our will,)
We, out of our free bounties, will deliver
The motives that divert[1] us. You well know
That, three years since, to our much grief, we lost
Our duchess; such a duchess, that the world,
In her whole course of life[2], yields not a lady
That can with imitation deserve
To be her second; in her grave we buried
All thoughts of woman: let this satisfy
For any second marriage. Now, whereas

You name the heir of Urbin, as a princess
Of great revenues, 'tis confess'd she is so:
But for some causes, private to ourself,
We have disposed her otherwise. Yet despair not;
For you, ere long, with joy shall understand,
That in our princely care we have provided
One worthy to succeed us.

[Enter **SANAZARRO**.

HIPPOLITO
We submit,
And hold the counsels of great Cozimo
Oraculous.

COZIMO
My Sanazarro!—Nay,
Forbear all ceremony. You look sprightly, friend,
And promise in your clear aspect some novel
That may delight us.

SANAZARRO
O sir, I would not be
The harbinger of aught that might distaste you;
And therefore know (for 'twere a sin to torture
Your highness' expectation) your vice-admiral,
By my directions, hath surprised the galleys
Appointed to transport the Asian tribute
Of the great Turk. A richer prize was never
Brought into Florence.

COZIMO
Still my nightingale,
That with sweet accents dost assure me that
My spring of happiness comes fast upon me!
Embrace me boldly. I pronounce that wretch
An enemy to brave and thriving action,
That dares believe but in a thought, we are
Too prodigal in our favours to this man,
Whose merits, though with him we should divide
Our dukedom, still continue us his debtor.

HIPPOLITO
'Tis far from me.

ALPHONSO
We all applaud it.

COZIMO
Nay, blush not, Sanazarro; we are proud
Of what we build up in thee; nor can our
Election be disparaged, since we have not
Received into our bosom and our grace
A glorious[3] lazy drone, grown fat with feeding
On others' toil, but an industrious bee,
That crops the sweet flowers of our enemies,
And every happy evening returns
Loaden with wax and honey to our hive.

SANAZARRO
My best endeavours never can discharge
The service I should pay.

COZIMO
Thou art too modest;
But we will study how to give, and when,

[Enter **GIOVANNI** and **CONTARINO**.

Before it be demanded.—Giovanni!
My nephew! let me eye thee better, boy.
In thee, methinks, my sister lives again;
For her love I will be a father to thee,
For thou art my adopted son.

GIOVANNI
Your servant,
And humblest subject.

COZIMO
Thy hard travel, nephew,
Requires soft rest, and therefore we forbear,
For the present, an account how thou hast spent
Thy absent hours. See, signiors, see, our care,
Without a second bed, provides you of
A hopeful prince. Carry him to his lodgings,
And, for his further honour, Sanazarro,
With the rest, do you attend him.

GIOVANNI
All true pleasures
Circle your highness!

SANAZARRO
As the rising sun,
We do receive you.

GIOVANNI
May this never set,
But shine upon you ever!

[Exeunt **GIOVANNI, SANAZARRO, HIERONIMO, ALPHONSO**, and **HIPPOLITO**.

COZIMO
Contarino!

CONTARINO
My gracious lord.

COZIMO
What entertainment found you
From Carolo de Charomonte?

CONTARINO
Free,
And bountiful. He's ever like himself,
Noble and hospitable.

COZIMO
But did my nephew
Depart thence willingly?

CONTARINO
He obey'd your summons
As did become him. Yet it was apparent,
But that he durst not cross your will, he would
Have sojourn'd longer there, he ever finding
Variety of sweetest entertainment.
But there was something else; nor can I blame
His youth, though with some trouble he took leave
Of such a sweet companion.

COZIMO
Who was it?

CONTARINO
The daughter, sir, of signior Carolo,
Fair Lidia, a virgin, at all parts,
But in her birth and fortunes, equal to him.
The rarest beauties Italy can make boast of
Are but mere shadows to her, she the substance
Of all perfection. And what increases
The wonder, sir, her body's matchless form
Is better'd by the pureness of her soul.

Such sweet discourse, such ravishing behaviour,
Such charming language, such enchanting manners,
With a simplicity that shames all courtship[4],
Flow hourly from her, that I do believe
Had Circe or Calypso her sweet graces,
Wandering Ulysses never had remember'd
Penelope, or Ithaca.

COZIMO
Be not rapt so.

CONTARINO
Your excellence would be so, had you seen her.

COZIMO
Take up, take up[5].—But did your observation
Note any passage of affection
Between her and my nephew?

CONTARINO
How it should
Be otherwise between them, is beyond
My best imagination. Cupid's arrows
Were useless there; for of necessity,
Their years and dispositions do accord so,
They must wound one another.

COZIMO
Umph! Thou art
My secretary, Contarino, and more skill'd
In politic designs of state, than in
Thy judgment of a beauty; give me leave,
In this, to doubt it.—Here. Go to my cabinet,
You shall find there letters newly received,
Touching the state of Urbin.
Pray you, with care peruse them: leave the search
Of this to us.

CONTARINO
I do obey in all things.

[Exit.

COZIMO
Lidia! a diamond so long conceal'd,
And never worn in court! of such sweet feature!
And he on whom I fix my dukedom's hopes
Made captive to it! Umph! 'tis somewhat strange.

Our eyes are every where, and we will make
A strict inquiry.—Sanazarro!

[Re-enter **SANAZARRO**.

SANAZARRO
Sir.

COZIMO
Is my nephew at his rest?

SANAZARRO
I saw him in bed, sir.

COZIMO
'Tis well; and does the princess Fiorinda,
Nay, do not blush, she is rich Urbin's heir,
Continue constant in her favours to you?

SANAZARRO
Dread sir, she may dispense them as she pleases;
But I look up to her as on a princess
I dare not be ambitious of, and hope
Her prodigal graces shall not render me
Offender to your highness.

COZIMO
Not a scruple.
He whom I favour, as I do my friend,
May take all lawful graces that become him:
But touching this hereafter. I have now
(And though perhaps it may appear a trifle)
Serious employment for thee.

SANAZARRO
I stand ready
For any act you please.

COZIMO
I know it, friend.
Have you ne'er heard of Lidia, the daughter
Of Carolo Charomonte?

SANAZARRO
Him I know, sir,
For a noble gentleman, and my worthy friend;
But never heard of her.

COZIMO
She is deliver'd,
And feelingly to us, by Contarino,
For a masterpiece in nature. I would have you
Ride suddenly thither to behold this wonder,
But not as sent by us; that's our first caution:
The second is, and carefully observe it,
That, though you are a bachelor, and endow'd with
All those perfections that may take a virgin,
On forfeit of our favour do not tempt her:
It may be her fair graces do concern us.
Pretend what business you think fit, to gain
Access unto her father's house, and, there,
Make full discovery of her, and return me
A true relation:—I have some ends in it,
With which we will acquaint you.

SANAZARRO
This is, sir,
An easy task.

COZIMO
Yet one that must exact
Your secrecy and diligence. Let not
Your stay be long.

SANAZARRO
It shall not, sir.

COZIMO
Farewell,
And be, as you would keep our favour, careful.

[Exeunt.

FOOTNOTES

[1] Divert us.] i. e. turn us aside from following your advice.

[2] —that the world,
In her whole course of life, &c.]
This is awkwardly expressed, a circumstance most unusual with Massinger; but seems to mean, in her various excellences and virtues.—GIFFORD.

[3] Glorious,] i. e. vain, empty, vaunting.

[4] All courtship,] i. e. all court breeding.

[5] *Take up, take up.] i. e. stop, check yourself.*

SCENE I

The Same. A Room in Fiorinda's House.

Enter **FIORINDA** and **CALAMINTA**.

FIORINDA
How does this dressing show?

CALAMINTA
'Tis of itself
Curious and rare; but, borrowing ornament,
As it does from your grace, that deigns to wear it,
Incomparable.

FIORINDA
Thou flatter'st me.

CALAMINTA
I cannot,
Your excellence is above it.

FIORINDA
Were we less perfect,
Yet, being as we are, an absolute princess,
We of necessity must be chaste, wise, fair,
By our prerogative!—yet all these fail
To move where I would have them. How received
Count Sanazarro the rich scarf I sent him
For his last visit?

CALAMINTA
With much reverence,
I dare not say affection. He express'd
More ceremony in his humble thanks,
Than feeling of the favour; and appear'd
Wilfully ignorant, in my opinion,
Of what it did invite him to.

FIORINDA
No matter;

He's blind with too much light[1]. Have you not heard
Of any private mistress he's engaged to?

CALAMINTA
Not any; and this does amaze me, madam,
That he, a soldier, should in his manners
Be so averse to women.

FIORINDA
Troth, I know not.

CALAMINTA
I do suspect him; for I learnt last night,
When the great duke went to rest, attended by
One private follower, he took horse; but whither
He's rid, or to what end, I cannot guess at,
But I will find it out.

FIORINDA
Do, faithful servant;

[Enter **CALANDRINO**.

We would not be abused.—Who have we here?

CALAMINTA
How the fool stares!

FIORINDA
And looks as if he were
Conning his neck-verse.

CALANDRINO
If I now prove perfect
In my A B C of courtship, Calandrino
Is made for ever. I am sent—let me see,
On a How d'ye, as they call 't.

CALAMINTA
What wouldst thou say?

CALANDRINO
Let me see my notes. These are her lodgings; well.

CALAMINTA
Art thou an ass?

CALANDRINO

Peace! thou art a court wagtail,

[Looking on his instructions.

To interrupt me.

FIORINDA
He has given it you.

CALANDRINO
And then say to the illustrious Fi-o-rin-da—
I have it. Which is she?

CALAMINTA
Why this; fop-doodle.

CALANDRINO
Leave chattering, bull-finch; you would put me out,
But 'twill not do.—Then, after you have made
Your three obeisances to her, kneel, and kiss
The skirt of her gown.—I am glad it is no worse.

CALAMINTA
This is sport unlook'd for.

CALANDRINO
Are you the princess?

FIORINDA
Yes, sir.

CALANDRINO
Then stand fair,
For I am choleric; and do not nip
A hopeful blossom. Out again:—Three low
Obeisances—

FIORINDA
I am ready.

CALANDRINO
I come on, then.

CALAMINTA
With much formality.

CALANDRINO
Umph! One, two, three.

[Makes antic courtesies.

Thus far I am right. Now for the last.

[Kisses the skirt of her gown.]

—O, rare!
She is perfumed all over! Sure great women,
Instead of little dogs, are privileged
To carry musk-cats.

FIORINDA
Now the ceremony
Is pass'd, what is the substance?

CALANDRINO
I'll peruse
My instructions, and then tell you.—Her skirt kiss'd,
Inform her highness that your lord—

CALAMINTA
Who's that?

CALANDRINO
Prince Giovanni, who entreats your grace,
That he, with your good favour, may have leave
To present his service to you. I think I have nick'd it
For a courtier of the first form.

FIORINDA
To my wonder.

[Enter **GIOVANNI** and a **GENTLEMAN**.

Return unto the prince—but he prevents
My answer. Calaminta, take him off;
And, for the neat delivery of his message,
Give him ten ducats: such rare parts as yours
Are to be cherish'd.

CALANDRINO
We will share: I know
It is the custom of the court, when ten
Are promised, five is fair. Fie! fie! the princess
Shall never know it, so you despatch me quickly,
And bid me not come to-morrow.

CALAMINTA
Very good, sir.

[Exeunt **CALANDRINO** and **CALAMINTA**.

GIOVANNI
Pray you, friend,
Inform the duke I am putting into act
What he commanded.

GENTLEMAN
I am proud to be employ'd, sir.

[Exit.

GIOVANNI
Madam, that, without warrant, I presume
To trench upon your privacies, may argue
Rudeness of manners; but the free access
Your princely courtesy vouchsafes to all
That come to pay their services, gives me hope
To find a gracious pardon.

FIORINDA
If you please, not
To make that an offence in your construction,
Which I receive as a large favour from you,
There needs not this apology.

GIOVANNI
You continue,
As you were ever, the greatest mistress of
Fair entertainment.

FIORINDA
You are, sir, the master;
And in the country have learnt to outdo
All that in court is practised. But why should we
Talk at such distance? You are welcome, sir.
We have been more familiar, and since
You will impose the province (you should govern)
Of boldness on me, give me leave to say
You are too punctual. Sit, sir, and discourse
As we were used.

GIOVANNI
Your excellence knows so well

How to command, that I can never err
When I obey you.

FIORINDA
Nay, no more of this.
You shall o'ercome; no more, I pray you, sir.—
And what delights, pray you be liberal
In your relation, hath the country life
Afforded you?

GIOVANNI
All pleasures, gracious madam,
But the happiness to converse with your sweet virtues.
I had a grave instructor, and my hours
Design'd to serious studies yielded me
Pleasure with profit, in the knowledge of
What before I was ignorant in; the signior,
Carolo de Charomonte, being skilful
To guide me through the labyrinth of wild passions,
That labour'd to imprison my free soul
A slave to vicious sloth.

FIORINDA
You speak him well.

GIOVANNI
But short of his deserts. Then for the time
Of recreation, I was allow'd
(Against the form follow'd by jealous parents
In Italy) full liberty to partake
His daughter's sweet society. She's a virgin
Happy in all endowments which a poet
Could fancy in his mistress; being herself
A school of goodness, where chaste maids may learn,
Without the aids of foreign principles,
By the example of her life and pureness,
To be as she is, excellent. I but give you
A brief epitome of her virtues, which,
Dilated on at large, and to their merit,
Would make an ample story.

FIORINDA
Your whole age,
So spent with such a father, and a daughter,
Could not be tedious to you.

GIOVANNI
True, great princess:

And now, since you have pleased to grant the hearing
Of my time's expense in the country, give me leave
To entreat the favour to be made acquainted
What service, or what objects in the court,
Have, in your excellency's acceptance, proved
Most gracious to you.

FIORINDA
I'll meet your demand,
And make a plain discovery. The duke's care
For my estate and person holds the first
And choicest place: then, the respect the courtiers
Pay gladly to me, not to be contemn'd.
But that which raised in me the most delight,
(For I am a friend to valour,) was to hear
The noble actions truly reported
Of the brave count Sanazarro. I profess,
When it hath been, and fervently, deliver'd,
How boldly, in the horror of a fight,
Cover'd with fire and smoke, and, as if nature
Had lent him wings, like lightning he hath fallen
Upon the Turkish galleys, I have heard it
With a kind of pleasure, which hath whisper'd to me,
This worthy must be cherish'd.

GIOVANNI
'Twas a bounty
You never can repent.

FIORINDA
I glory in it.
And when he did return, (but still with conquest,)
His armour off, not young Antinous
Appear'd more courtly; all the graces that
Render a man's society dear to ladies,
Like pages waiting on him; and it does
Work strangely on me.

GIOVANNI
To divert your thoughts,
Though they are fix'd upon a noble subject,
I am a suitor to you.

FIORINDA
You will ask,
I do presume, what I may grant, and then
It must not be denied.

GIOVANNI
It is a favour
For which I hope your excellence will thank me.

FIORINDA
Nay, without circumstance.

GIOVANNI
That you would please
To take occasion to move the duke,
That you, with his allowance, may command
This matchless virgin, Lidia, (of whom
I cannot speak too much,) to wait upon you.
She's such a one, upon the forfeit of
Your good opinion of me, that will not
Be a blemish to your train.

FIORINDA
'Tis rank! he loves her:
But I will fit him with a suit. [Aside.]—I pause not,
As if it bred or doubt or scruple in me
To do what you desire, for I'll effect it,
And make use of a fair and fit occasion;
Yet, in return, I ask a boon of you,
And hope to find you, in your grant to me,
As I have been to you.

GIOVANNI
Command me, madam.

FIORINDA
'Tis near allied to yours. That you would be
A suitor to the duke, not to expose,
After so many trials of his faith,
The noble Sanazarro to all dangers,
As if he were a wall to stand the fury
Of a perpetual battery: but now
To grant him, after his long labours, rest
And liberty to live in court; his arms
And his victorious sword and shield hung up
For monuments.

GIOVANNI
Umph!—I'll embrace, fair princess,

[Enter **COZIMO**.

The soonest opportunity. The duke!

COZIMO
Nay, blush not; we smile on your privacy,
And come not to disturb you. You are equals,
And, without prejudice to either's honours,
May make a mutual change of love and courtship,
Till you are made one, and with holy rites,
And we give suffrage to it.

GIOVANNI
You are gracious.

COZIMO
To ourself in this: but now break off; too much
Taken at once of the most curious viands,
Dulls the sharp edge of appetite. We are now
For other sports, in which our pleasure is
That you should keep us company.

FIORINDA
We attend you.

[Exeunt.

FOOTNOTE:

[1] He's blind with too much light.] Ennobled by Milton—"dark with excess of light."

SCENE II

The Country. A Hall in Charamonte's House.

Enter **BERNARDO, CAPONI,** and **PETRUCHIO.**

BERNARDO
Is my lord stirring?

CAPONI
No; he's fast.

PETRUCHIO
Let us take, then,
Our morning draught. Such as eat store of beef,
Mutton, and capons, may preserve their healths
With that thin composition call'd small beer,

As, 'tis said, they do in England. But Italians,
That think when they have supp'd upon an olive,
A root, or bunch of raisins, 'tis a feast,
Must kill those crudities rising from cold herbs,
With hot and lusty wines.

CAPONI
A happiness
Those tramontanes[1] ne'er tasted.

BERNARDO
Have they not
Store of wine there?

CAPONI
Yes, and drink more in two hours
Than the Dutchmen or the Dane in four and twenty.

PETRUCHIO
But what is 't? French trash, made of rotten grapes,
And dregs and lees of Spain, with Welsh metheglin,
A drench to kill a horse! But this pure nectar,
Being proper to our climate, is too fine
To brook the roughness of the sea: the spirit
Of this begets in us quick apprehensions,
And active executions; whereas their
Gross feeding makes their understanding like it:
They can fight, and that's their all.

[They drink.

[Enter **SANAZARRO** and **SERVANT**.

SANAZARRO
Security
Dwells about this house, I think; the gate's wide open,
And not a servant stirring. See the horses
Set up, and clothed.

SERVANT
I shall, sir.

[Exit.

SANAZARRO
I'll make bold
To press a little further.

BERNARDO
Who is this,
Count Sanazarro?

PETRUCHIO
Yes, I know him. Quickly
Remove the flagon.

SANAZARRO
A good day to you, friends.
Nay, do not conceal your physic; I approve it,
And, if you please, will be a patient with you.

PETRUCHIO
My noble lord.

[Drinks.

SANAZARRO
A health to yours.

[Drinks.]

Well done!
I see you love yourselves, and I commend you;
'Tis the best wisdom.

PETRUCHIO
May it please your honour
To walk a turn in the gallery, I'll acquaint
My lord with your being here.

[Exit.

SANAZARRO
Tell him I come
For a visit only. 'Tis a handsome pile this.

[Exit.

CAPONI
Why here is a brave fellow, and a right one;
Nor wealth nor greatness makes him proud.

BERNARDO
There are
Too few of them; for most of our new courtiers,
(Whose fathers were familiar with the prices

Of oil and corn, with when and where to vent them,
And left their heirs rich, from their knowledge that way,)
Like gourds shot up in a night, disdain to speak
But to cloth of tissue.

[Enter **CHAROMONTE** in a nightgown, **PETRUCHIO** following.

CHAROMONTE
Stand you prating, knaves,
When such a guest is under my roof! See all
The rooms perfumed. This is the man that carries
The sway and swing of the court; and I had rather
Preserve him mine with honest offices, than—
But I'll make no comparisons. Bid my daughter
Trim herself up to the height. Which way went he?

CAPONI
To the round gallery.

CHAROMONTE
I will entertain him
As fits his worth and quality, but no further.

[Exeunt.

FOOTNOTE

[1] Tramontanes,] i. e. strangers, barbarians: so the Italians called, and still call, all who live beyond the Alps, ultra montes. In a subsequent speech, the author does not forget to satirize the acknowledged propensity of his countrymen to drinking: "Your Dane, your German, and your swag-bellied Hollander, are nothing to your Englishman."

If Caponi, as well as Iago, be not, however, too severe upon us, it must be confessed that our ancestors were apt scholars, and soon bettered the instructions which they received. Sir Richard Baker (as Mr. Gilchrist observes), treating of the wars in the Low-Countries about the end of the sixteenth century, says, "Here it must not be omitted, that the English (who, of all the dwellers in the northern parts of the world, were hitherto the least drinkers, and deservedly praised for their sobriety) in these Dutch wars learned to be drunkards, and brought the vice so far to overspread the kingdom, that laws were fain to be enacted for repressing it." Chron. fol. p. 382.—GIFFORD.

SCENE III

A Gallery in the Same.

Enter **SANAZARRO**.

SANAZARRO
I cannot apprehend, yet I have argued
All ways I can imagine, for what reasons
The great duke does employ me hither; and,
What does increase the miracle, I must render
A strict and true account, at my return,
Of Lidia, this lord's daughter, and describe
In what she's excellent, and where defective.
'Tis a hard task: he that will undergo
To make a judgment of a woman's beauty,
And see through all her plasterings and paintings,
Had need of Lynceus' eyes, and with more ease
May look, like him, through nine mud walls, than make
A true discovery of her. But the intents
And secrets of my prince's heart must be
Served, and not search'd into.

[Enter **CHAROMONTE**.

CHAROMONTE
Most noble sir,
Excuse my age, subject to ease and sloth,
That with no greater speed I have presented
My service with your welcome.

SANAZARRO
'Tis more fit
That I should ask your pardon, for disturbing
Your rest at this unseasonable hour.
But my occasions carrying me so near
Your hospitable house, my stay being short too,
Your goodness, and the name of friend, which you
Are pleased to grace me with, gave me assurance
A visit would not offend.

CHAROMONTE
Offend, my lord!
I feel myself much younger for the favour.
How is it with our gracious master?

SANAZARRO
He, sir,
Holds still his wonted greatness, and confesses
Himself your debtor, for your love and care
To the prince Giovanni; and had sent
Particular thanks by me, had his grace known
The quick despatch of what I was design'd to

Would have licensed me to see you.

CHAROMONTE
I am rich
In his acknowledgment.

SANAZARRO
I have heard
Your happiness in a daughter.

CHAROMONTE
Sits the wind there? [Aside.

SANAZARRO
Fame gives her out for a rare masterpiece.

CHAROMONTE
'Tis a plain village girl, sir, but obedient;
That's her best beauty, sir.

SANAZARRO
Let my desire
To see her find a fair construction from you:
I bring no loose thought with me.

CHAROMONTE
You are that way,
My lord, free from suspicion. Her own manners,
Without an imposition from me,
I hope, will prompt her to it.

[Enter **LIDIA** and **PETRONELLA**.

As she is,
She comes to make a tender of that service
Which she stands bound to pay.

SANAZARRO
With your fair leave,
I make bold to salute you.

LIDIA
Sir, you have it.

CHAROMONTE
How he falls off!

LIDIA

My lord, though silence best becomes a maid,
And to be curious to know but what
Concerns myself, and with becoming distance,
May argue me of boldness, I must borrow
So much of modesty, as to inquire
Prince Giovanni's health.

SANAZARRO
He cannot want
What you are pleased to wish him.

LIDIA
Would 'twere so!
And then there is no blessing that can make
A hopeful and a noble prince complete,
But should fall on him. O! he was our north star,
The light and pleasure of our eyes.

SANAZARRO
Where am I?
I feel myself another thing! Can charms
Be writ on such pure rubies[1]? her lips melt
As soon as touch'd! Not those smooth gales that glide
O'er happy Araby, or rich Sabæa,
Creating in their passage gums and spices,
Can serve for a weak simile to express
The sweetness of her breath. Such a brave stature
Homer bestow'd on Pallas, every limb
Proportion'd to it!

CHAROMONTE
This is strange.—My lord!

SANAZARRO
I crave your pardon, and yours, matchless maid,
For such I must report you.

PETRONELLA
There's no notice
Taken all this while of me.   [Aside.

SANAZARRO
And I must add,
If your discourse and reason parallel
The rareness of your more than human form,
You are a wonder.

CHAROMONTE

Pray you, my lord, make trial:
She can speak, I can assure you; and that my presence
May not take from her freedom, I will leave you:
For know, my lord, my confidence dares trust her
Where, and with whom, she pleases.—Petronella!

PETRONELLA
Yes, my good lord.

CHAROMONTE
I have employment for you.

[Exeunt **CHAROMONTE** and **PETRONELLA**.

LIDIA
What's your will, sir?

SANAZARRO
Madam, you are so large a theme to treat of,
And every grace about you offers to me
Such copiousness of language, that I stand
Doubtful which first to touch at. If I err,
As in my choice I may, let me entreat you,
Before I do offend, to sign my pardon:
Let this, the emblem of your innocence,
Give me assurance.

LIDIA
My hand join'd to yours,
Without this superstition, confirms it.
Nor need I fear you will dwell long upon me,
The barrenness of the subject yielding nothing
That rhetoric, with all her tropes and figures,
Can amplify. Yet since you are resolved
To prove yourself a courtier in my praise,
As I'm a woman (and you men affirm
Our sex loves to be flatter'd) I'll endure it.

[Enter **CHAROMONTE** above.

Now, when you please, begin.

SANAZARRO [Turning from her]
If the great duke
Made this his end to try my constant temper,
Though I am vanquished, 'tis his fault, not mine;
For I am flesh and blood, and have affections
Like other men. Who can behold the temples,

Or holy altars, but the objects work
Devotion in him? And I may as well
Walk over burning iron with bare feet,
And be unscorch'd, as look upon this beauty
Without desire, and that desire pursued too,
Till it be quench'd with the enjoying those
Delights, which to achieve, danger is nothing,
And loyalty but a word.

LIDIA
I ne'er was proud;
Nor can find I am guilty of a thought
Deserving this neglect.

SANAZARRO
Suppose his greatness
Loves her himself, why makes he choice of me
To be his agent? It is tyranny
To call one pinch'd with hunger to a feast,
And at that instant cruelly deny him
To taste of what he sees. Allegiance
Tempted too far is like the trial of
A good sword on an anvil; as that often
Flies in pieces without service to the owner,
So trust enforced too far proves treachery,
And is too late repented.

LIDIA
Pray you, sir,
Or license me to leave you, or deliver
The reasons which invite you to command
My tedious waiting on you.

CHAROMONTE
As I live,
I know not what to think on 't. Is 't his pride,
Or his simplicity?

SANAZARRO
Whither have my thoughts
Carried me from myself? In this my dulness,
I've lost an opportunity—

[Turns to her; she falls off.

LIDIA
'Tis true
I was not bred in court, nor live a star there;

Nor shine in rich embroideries and pearl,
As they that are the mistresses of great fortunes
Are every day adorn'd with—

SANAZARRO
Will you vouchsafe
Your ear, sweet lady?

LIDIA
Yet I may be bold,
For my integrity and fame, to rank
With such as are more glorious. Though I never
Did injury, yet I am sensible
When I'm contemn'd and scorn'd.

SANAZARRO
Will you please to hear me?

LIDIA
O the difference of natures! Giovanni,
A prince in expectation, when he lived here,
Stole courtesy from heaven[2], and would not to
The meanest servant in my father's house
Have kept such distance.

SANAZARRO
Pray you, do not think me
Unworthy of your ear: it was your beauty
That turn'd me statue. I can speak, fair lady.

LIDIA
And I can hear. The harshness of your courtship
Cannot corrupt my courtesy.

SANAZARRO
Will you hear me,
If I speak of love?

LIDIA
Provided you be modest;
I were uncivil, else.

CHAROMONTE
They are come to parley:
I must observe this nearer.

[He retires.

SANAZARRO

You are a rare one,
And such (but that my haste commands me hence)
I could converse with ever. Will you grace me
With leave to visit you again?

LIDIA

So you,
At your return to court, do me the favour
To make a tender of my humble service
To the prince Giovanni.

SANAZARRO

Ever touching
Upon that string! [Aside.]
And will you give me hope
Of future happiness?

LIDIA

That, as I shall find you:
The fort that's yielded at the first assault
Is hardly worth the taking.

[Re-enter **CHAROMONTE** below.

SANAZARRO

She is a magazine of all perfection,
And 'tis death to part from her, yet I must.

CHAROMONTE

A homely breakfast does attend your lordship,
Such as the place affords.

SANAZARRO

No; I have feasted
Already here; my thanks, and so I leave you:
I will see you again.—Till this unhappy hour
I was never lost; and what to do, or say,
I have not yet determined.

[Aside, and exit.

CHAROMONTE

Gone so abruptly!
'Tis very strange.

LIDIA

Under your favour, sir,

His coming hither was to little purpose,
For any thing I heard from him.

CHAROMONTE
Take heed, Lidia!
I do advise you with a father's love,
And tenderness of your honour; as I would not
Have you too harsh in giving entertainment,
So by no means be credulous: for great men,
Till they have gain'd their ends, are giants in
Their promises, but, those obtain'd, weak pigmies
In their performance. And it is a maxim
Allow'd among them, so they may deceive,
They may swear any thing; for the queen of love,
As they hold constantly, does never punish,
But smile at, lovers' perjuries[3].—Yet be wise too,
And when you are sued to in a noble way,
Be neither nice nor scrupulous.

LIDIA
All you speak, sir,
I hear as oracles; nor will digress
From your directions.

CHAROMONTE
So shall you keep Your fame untainted.

LIDIA
As I would my life, sir.

[Exeunt.

FOOTNOTES

[1] —Can charms
Be writ on such pure rubies?]
This, I believe, alludes to a very old opinion, that some sorts of gems (from an inherent sanctity) could
not be profaned, or applied to the purposes of magic. The notion took its rise probably from some
superstitious ideas respecting the precious stones employed in the breastplate of the high-priest of the
Jews.—GIFFORD.

[2] Stole courtesy from heaven.] This is from Shakspeare; and the plain meaning of the phrase is, that the
affability and sweetness of Giovanni were of a heavenly kind.—GIFFORD.

[3] Smile at lovers' perjuries.]

Ridet hoc, inquam, Venus ipsa.

It would be as well if the queen of love had been a little more fastidious on this subject. Her facility, I fear, has done much mischief, as lovers of all ages have availed themselves of it: but she had it from her father, whose laxity of principle is well known:

—perjuria ridet amantûm
Jupiter.
GIFFORD.

ACT III

SCENE I

Florence. An Ante-room in the Palace.

Enter **SANAZARRO** and **SERVANT**.

SANAZARRO
Leave the horses with my grooms; but be you careful,
With your best diligence and speed, to find out
The prince, and humbly, in my name, entreat
I may exchange some private conference with him
Before the great duke know of my arrival.

SERVANT
I haste, my lord.

SANAZARRO
Here I'll attend his coming:
And see you keep yourself, as much as may be,
Conceal'd from all men else.

SERVANT
To serve your lordship,
I wish I were invisible.

[Exit.

SANAZARRO
I am driven
Into a desperate strait, and cannot steer
A middle course; and of the two extremes
Which I must make election of, I know not
Which is more full of horror. Never servant
Stood more engaged to a magnificent master,
Than I to Cozimo: and all those honours

And glories by his grace conferr'd upon me,
Or by my prosperous services deserved,
If now I should deceive his trust, and make
A shipwreck of my loyalty, are ruin'd.
And, on the other side, if I discover
Lidia's divine perfections, all my hopes
In her are sunk, never to be buoy'd up:
For 'tis impossible, but, as soon as seen,
She must with adoration be sued to.
A hermit at his beads but looking on her
At this object would take fire. Nor is the duke
Such an Hippolytus, but that this Phædra,
But seen, must force him to forsake the groves
And Dian's huntmanship, proud to serve under
Venus' soft ensigns. No, there is no way
For me to hope fruition of my ends,
But to conceal her beauties;—and how that
May be effected is as hard a task
As with a veil to cover the sun's beams,
Or comfortable light. Three years the prince
Lived in her company, and Contarino,
The secretary, hath possess'd[1] the duke
What a rare piece she is:—but he's my creature,
And may with ease be frighted to deny
What he hath said: and if my long experience,
With some strong reasons I have thought upon,
Cannot o'er-reach a youth, my practice yields me
But little profit.

[Enter **GIOVANNI** with the **SERVANT**.

GIOVANNI
You are well return'd, sir.

SANAZARRO
Leave us.—

[Exit **SERVANT**.]

When that your grace shall know the motives
That forced me to invite you to this trouble,
You will excuse my manners.

GIOVANNI
Sir, there needs not
This circumstance between us. You are ever
My noble friend.

SANAZARRO

You shall have further cause
To assure you of my faith and zeal to serve you:
And when I have committed to your trust
(Presuming still on your retentive silence)
A secret of no less importance than
My honour, nay, my head, it will confirm
What value you hold with me.

GIOVANNI

Pray you, believe, sir,
What you deliver to me shall be lock'd up
In a strong cabinet, of which you yourself
Shall keep the key; for here I pawn my honour,
Which is the best security I can give yet,
It shall not be discover'd.

SANAZARRO

This assurance
Is more than I with modesty could demand
From such a paymaster; but I must be sudden;
And, therefore, to the purpose. Can your excellence,
In your imagination, conceive
On what design, or whither, the duke's will
Commanded me hence last night?

GIOVANNI

No, I assure you;
And it had been a rudeness to inquire
Of that I was not call'd to.

SANAZARRO

Grant me hearing,
And I will make you truly understand
It only did concern you.

GIOVANNI

Me, my lord!

SANAZARRO

You, in your present state and future fortunes;
For both lie at the stake.

GIOVANNI

You much amaze me.
Pray you, resolve this riddle.

SANAZARRO

You know the duke,
If he die issueless, as yet he is,
Determines you his heir.

GIOVANNI
It hath pleased his highness
Oft to profess so much.

SANAZARRO
But say he should
Be won to prove a second wife, on whom
He may beget a son, how, in a moment,
Will all those glorious expectations, which
Render you reverenced and remarkable,
Be in a moment blasted, howe'er you are
His much-loved sister's son!

GIOVANNI
I must bear it
With patience, and in me it is a duty
That I was born with; and 'twere much unfit
For the receiver of a benefit
To offer, for his own ends, to prescribe
Laws to the giver's pleasure.

SANAZARRO
Sweetly answer'd,
And like your noble self. This your rare temper
So wins upon me, that I would not live
(If that by honest arts I can prevent it)
To see your hopes made frustrate. And but think
How you shall be transform'd from what you are,
Should this (as Heaven avert it!) ever happen.
It must disturb your peace: for whereas now,
Being, as you are, received for the heir-apparent,
You are no sooner seen but wonder'd at;
The signiors making it a business to
Inquire how you have slept; and, as you walk
The streets of Florence, the glad multitude
In throngs press but to see you; and, with joy,
The father, pointing with his finger, tells
His son, This is the prince, the hopeful prince,
That must hereafter rule, and you obey him.—
Great ladies beg your picture, and make love
To that, despairing to enjoy the substance.—
And but the last night, when 'twas only rumour'd
That you were come to court, as if you had
By sea pass'd hither from another world,

What general shouts and acclamations follow'd!
The bells rang loud, the bonfires blazed, and such
As loved not wine, carousing to your health,
Were drunk, and blush'd not at it. And is this
A happiness to part with?

GIOVANNI
I allow these
As flourishes of fortune, with which princes
Are often soothed; but never yet esteem'd them
For real blessings.

SANAZARRO
Yet all these were paid
To what you may be, not to what you are;
For if the Great Duke but show to his servants
A son of his own, you shall, like one obscure,
Pass unregarded.

GIOVANNI
I confess, command
Is not to be contemn'd, and if my fate
Appoint me to it, as I may, I'll bear it
With willing shoulders. But, my lord, as yet,
You've told me of a danger coming towards me,
But have not named it.

SANAZARRO
That is soon deliver'd.
Great Cozimo, your uncle, as I more
Than guess, for 'tis no frivolous circumstance
That does persuade my judgment to believe it,
Purposes to be married.

GIOVANNI
Married, sir!
With whom, and on what terms? pray you, instruct me.

SANAZARRO
With the fair Lidia.

GIOVANNI
Lidia!

SANAZARRO
The daughter
Of signior Charomonte.

GIOVANNI
Pardon me
Though I appear incredulous; for, on
My knowledge, he ne'er saw her.

SANAZARRO
That is granted:
But Contarino hath so sung her praises,
And given her out for such a masterpiece,
That he's transported with it, sir:—and love
Steals sometimes through the ear into the heart,
As well as by the eye. The duke no sooner
Heard her described, but I was sent in post
To see her, and return my judgment of her.

GIOVANNI
And what's your censure[2]?

SANAZARRO
'Tis a pretty creature.

GIOVANNI
She's very fair.

SANAZARRO
Yes, yes, I have seen worse faces.

GIOVANNI
Her limbs are neatly form'd.

SANAZARRO
She hath a waist
Indeed sized to love's wish.

GIOVANNI
A delicate hand too.

SANAZARRO
Then for a leg and foot—

GIOVANNI
And there I leave you,
For I presumed no further.

SANAZARRO
As she is, sir,
I know she wants no gracious part that may
Allure the duke; and, if he only see her,

She is his own; he will not be denied,
And then you are lost: yet, if you'll second me,
(As you have reason, for it most concerns you,)
I can prevent all yet.

GIOVANNI
I would you could,
A noble way.

SANAZARRO
I will cry down her beauties;
Especially the beauties of her mind,
As much as Contarino hath advanced them;
And this, I hope, will breed forgetfulness,
And kill affection in him: but you must join
With me in my report, if you be question'd.

GIOVANNI
I never told a lie yet; and I hold it
In some degree blasphémous[3] to dispraise
What's worthy admiration: yet, for once,
I will dispraise a little, and not vary
From your relation.

SANAZARRO
Be constant in it.

[Enter **ALPHONSO**.

ALPHONSO
My lord, the duke hath seen your man, and wonders

[Enter **COZIMO, HIPPOLITO, CONTARINO**, and **ATTENDANTS**.

You come not to him. See, if his desire
To have conference with you hath not brought him hither
In his own person!

COZIMO
They are comely coursers,
And promise swiftness.

CONTARINO
They are, of my knowledge,
Of the best race in Naples.

COZIMO
You are, nephew,

As I hear, an excellent horseman, and we like it:
'Tis a fair grace in a prince. Pray you, make trial
Of their strength and speed; and, if you think them fit
For your employment, with a liberal hand
Reward the gentleman that did present them
From the viceroy of Naples.

GIOVANNI
I will use
My best endeavour, sir.

COZIMO
Wait on my nephew.

[Exeunt **GIOVANNI, ALPHONSO, HIPPOLITO,** and **ATTENDANTS.**

Nay, stay you, Contarino:—be within call;
It may be we shall use you.

[Exit **CONTARINO.**]

You have rode hard, sir,
And we thank you for it: every minute seems
Irksome, and tedious to us, till you have
Made your discovery. Say, friend, have you seen
This phoenix of our age?

SANAZARRO
I have seen a maid, sir;
But, if that I have judgment, no such wonder
As she was deliver'd to you.

COZIMO
This is strange.

SANAZARRO
But certain truth. It may be, she was look'd on
With admiration in the country, sir;
But, if compared with many in your court,
She would appear but ordinary.

COZIMO
Contarino
Reports her otherwise.

SANAZARRO
Such as ne'er saw swans
May think crows beautiful.

COZIMO
How is her behaviour?

SANAZARRO
'Tis like the place she lives in.

COZIMO
How her wit,
Discourse, and entertainment?

SANAZARRO
Very coarse;
I would not willingly say poor, and rude:
But, had she all the beauties of fair women,
The dulness of her soul would fright me from her.

COZIMO
You are curious, sir. I know not what to think on 't.—[Aside.
Contarino!

[Re-enter **CONTARINO**.

CONTARINO
Sir.

COZIMO
Where was thy judgment, man,
To extol a virgin Sanazarro tells me
Is nearer to deformity?

SANAZARRO
I saw her,
And curiously perused her; and I wonder
That she, that did appear to me, that know
What beauty is, not worthy the observing,
Should so transport you.

CONTARINO
Troth, my lord, I thought then—

COZIMO
Thought! Didst thou not affirm it?

CONTARINO
I confess, sir,
I did believe so then; but now I hear
My lord's opinion to the contrary,

I am of another faith: for 'tis not fit
That I should contradict him. I am dim, sir;
But he's sharp-sighted.

SANAZARRO
This is to my wish. [Aside.

COZIMO
We know not what to think of this; yet would not

[Re-enter **GIOVANNI**, **HIPPOLITO**, and **ALPHONSO**.

Determine rashly of it. [Aside.]—How do you like
My nephew's horsemanship?

HIPPOLITO
In my judgment, sir,
It is exact and rare.

ALPHONSO
And, to my fancy,
He did present great Alexander mounted
On his Bucephalus.

COZIMO
You are right, courtiers,
And know it is your duty to cry up
All actions of a prince.

SANAZARRO
Do not betray
Yourself, you're safe; I have done my part.
[Aside to **GIOVANNI**.

GIOVANNI
I thank you;
Nor will I fail.

COZIMO
What's your opinion, nephew,
Of the horses?

GIOVANNI
Two of them are, in my judgment,
The best I ever back'd; I mean the roan, sir,
And the brown bay: but for the chestnut-colour'd,
Though he be full of metal, hot, and fiery,
He treads weak in his pasterns.

COZIMO

So: come nearer;
This exercise hath put you into a sweat;
Take this and dry it: and now I command you
To tell me truly what's your censure of
Charomonte's daughter, Lidia.

GIOVANNI

I am, sir,
A novice in my judgment of a lady;
But such as 'tis, your grace shall have it freely.
I would not speak ill of her, and am sorry,
If I keep myself a friend to truth, I cannot
Report her as I would, so much I owe
Her reverend father: but I'll give you, sir,
As near as I can, her character in little.
She's of a goodly stature, and her limbs
Not disproportion'd; for her face, it is
Far from deformity; yet they flatter her,
That style it excellent: her manners are
Simple and innocent; but her discourse
And wit deserve my pity, more than praise:
At the best, my lord, she is a handsome picture,
And, that said, all is spoken.

COZIMO

I believe you;
I ne'er yet found you false.

GIOVANNI

Nor ever shall, sir.—
Forgive me, matchless Lidia! too much love,
And jealous fear to lose thee, do compel me,
Against my will, my reason, and my knowledge,
To be a poor detractor of that beauty,
Which fluent Ovid, if he lived again,
Would want words to express. [Aside.

COZIMO

Pray you, make choice of
The richest of our furniture for these horses,
[To **SANAZARRO.**
And take my nephew with you; we in this
Will follow his directions.

GIOVANNI

Could I find now

The princess Fiorinda, and persuade her
To be silent in the suit that I moved to her,
All were secure.

SANAZARRO
In that, my lord, I'll aid you.

COZIMO
We will be private; leave us.

[Exeunt all but **COZIMO**.

All my studies
And serious meditations aim no further
Than this young man's good. He was my sister's son,
And she was such a sister, when she lived,
I could not prize too much; nor can I better
Make known how dear I hold her memory,
Than in my cherishing the only issue
Which she hath left behind her. Who's that?

[Enter **FIORINDA**.

FIORINDA
Sir.

COZIMO
My fair charge! you are welcome to us.

FIORINDA
I have found it, sir.

COZIMO
All things go well in Urbin.

FIORINDA
Your gracious care to me, an orphan, frees me
From all suspicion that my jealous fears
Can drive into my fancy.

COZIMO
The next summer,
In our own person, we will bring you thither,
And seat you in your own.

FIORINDA
When you think fit, sir.
But, in the mean time, with your highness' pardon,

I am a suitor to you.

COZIMO
Name it, madam,
With confidence to obtain it.

FIORINDA
That you would please
To lay a strict command on Charomonte,
To bring his daughter Lidia to the court:
And pray you, think, sir, that 'tis not my purpose
To employ her as a servant, but to use her
As a most wish'd companion.

COZIMO
Ha! your reason?

FIORINDA
The hopeful prince, your nephew, sir, hath given her
To me for such an abstract of perfection
In all that can be wish'd for in a virgin,
As beauty, music, ravishing discourse,
Quickness of apprehension, with choice manners
And learning too, not usual with women,
That I am much ambitious (though I shall
Appear but as a foil to set her off)
To be by her instructed, and supplied
In what I am defective.

COZIMO
Did my nephew
Seriously deliver this?

FIORINDA
I assure your grace,
With zeal and vehemency; and, even when,
With his best words, he strived to set her forth,
(Though the rare subject made him eloquent,)
He would complain, all he could say came short
Of her deservings.

COZIMO
Pray you have patience.

[Walks aside.

This was strangely carried.—Ha! are we trifled with?
Dare they do this? Is Cozimo's fury, that

Of late was terrible, grown contemptible?
Well; we will clear our brows, and undermine
Their secret works, though they have digg'd like moles,
And crush them with the tempest of my wrath
When I appear most calm. He is unfit
To command others that knows not to use it[4],
And with all rigour: yet my stern looks shall not
Discover my intents; for I will strike
When I begin to frown.—You are the mistress
Of that you did demand.

FIORINDA
I thank your highness;
But speed in the performance of the grant
Doubles the favour, sir.

COZIMO
You shall possess it
Sooner than you expect:—
Only be pleased to be ready, when my secretary
Waits on you, to take the fresh air. My nephew,
And my bosom friend, so to cheat me! 'tis not fair. [Aside.

[Re-enter **GIOVANNI** and **SANAZARRO**.

SANAZARRO
Where should this princess be? nor in her lodgings,
Nor in the private walks, her own retreat,
Which she so much frequented!

GIOVANNI
By my life,
She's with the duke! and I much more than fear
Her forwardness to prefer my suit hath ruin'd
What with such care we built up.

COZIMO
Have you furnish'd
Those coursers, as we will'd you?

SANAZARRO
There's no sign
Of anger in his looks.

GIOVANNI
They are complete, sir.

COZIMO

'Tis well: to your rest. Soft sleeps wait on you, madam.
To-morrow, with the rising of the sun,
Be ready to ride with us.—They with more safety
Had trod on fork-tongued adders, than provoked me.

[Aside, and exit.

FIORINDA
I come not to be thank'd, sir, for the speedy
Performance of my promise touching Lidia:
It is effected.

SANAZARRO
We are undone. [Aside.

FIORINDA
The duke
No sooner heard me with my best of language
Describe her excellencies, as you taught me,
But he confirm'd it.—You look sad, as if
You wish'd it were undone.

GIOVANNI
No, gracious madam,
I am your servant for 't.

FIORINDA
Be you as careful
For what I moved to you.—Count Sanazarro,
Now I perceive you honour me, in vouchsafing
To wear so slight a favour.

SANAZARRO
'Tis a grace
I am unworthy of.

FIORINDA
You merit more,
In prizing so a trifle. Take this diamond;
I'll second what I have begun; for know,
Your valour hath so won upon me, that
'Tis not to be resisted: I have said, sir,
And leave you to interpret it.

[Exit.

SANAZARRO
This to me

Is wormwood. 'Tis apparent we are taken
In our own noose. What's to be done?

GIOVANNI
I know not.
And 'tis a punishment justly fallen upon me,
For leaving truth, a constant mistress, that
Ever protects her servants, to become
A slave to lies and falsehood. What excuse
Can we make to the duke, what mercy hope for,
Our packing[5] being laid open?

SANAZARRO
'Tis not to
Be question'd but his purposed journey is
To see fair Lidia.

GIOVANNI
And to divert him
Impossible.

SANAZARRO
There's now no looking backward.

GIOVANNI
And which way to go on with safety, not
To be imagined.

SANAZARRO
Give me leave: I have
An embryon in my brain, which, I despair not,
May be brought to form and fashion, provided
You will be open-breasted.

GIOVANNI
'Tis no time now,
Our dangers being equal, to conceal
A thought from you.

SANAZARRO
What power hold you o'er Lidia?
Do you think that, with some hazard of her life,
She would prevent your ruin?

GIOVANNI
I presume so:
If, in the undertaking it, she stray not
From what becomes her innocence; and to that

'Tis far from me to press her: I myself
Will rather suffer.

SANAZARRO
'Tis enough; this night
Write to her by your servant Calandrino,
As I shall give directions; my man

[Enter **CALANDRINO**, fantastically dressed.

Shall bear him company. See, sir, to my wish
He does appear; but much transform'd from what
He was when he came hither.

CALANDRINO
I confess
I am not very wise, and yet I find
A fool, so he be parcel knave, in court
May flourish and grow rich.

GIOVANNI
Calandrino.

CALANDRINO
Peace!
I am in contemplation.

GIOVANNI
Do not you know me?

CALANDRINO
I tell thee, no; on forfeit of my place,
I must not know myself, much less my father,
But by petition; that petition lined too
With golden birds, that sing to the tune of profit,
Or I am deaf.

GIOVANNI
But you've your sense of feeling.

[Offering to strike him.

SANAZARRO
Nay, pray you, forbear.

CALANDRINO
I have all that's requisite
To the making up of a signior: my spruce ruff,

My hooded cloak, long stocking, and paned hose,
My case of toothpicks, and my silver fork[6];
To convey an olive neatly to my mouth;—
And, what is all in all, my pockets ring
A golden peal. O that the peasants in the country,
My quondam fellows, but saw me as I am,
How they would admire and worship me!

GIOVANNI
As they shall;
For instantly you must thither.

CALANDRINO
My grand signior,
Vouchsafe a beso las manos[7], and a cringe
Of the last edition.

GIOVANNI
You must ride post with letters
This night to Lidia.

CALANDRINO
An it please your grace,
Shall I use my coach, or footcloth mule?

SANAZARRO
You widgeon,
You are to make all speed; think not of pomp.

GIOVANNI
Follow for your instructions, sirrah.

CALANDRINO
I have
One suit to you, my good lord.

SANAZARRO
What is 't?

CALANDRINO
That you would give me
A subtile court-charm, to defend me from
The infectious air of the country.

GIOVANNI
What's the reason?

CALANDRINO

Why, as this court-air taught me knavish wit,
By which I am grown rich, if that again
Should turn me fool and honest, vain hopes farewell!
For I must die a beggar.

SANAZARRO
Go to, sirrah,
You'll be whipt for this.

GIOVANNI
Leave fooling, and attend us.

[Exeunt[8].

FOOTNOTES

[1] *Possessed,] i. e. informed.*

[2] *Censure,] i. e. judgment.*

[3] *Blasphémous.] So the word was usually accented in Massinger's time, and with strict regard to its Greek derivation.*

[4] *—that knows not to use it,]*
i. e. his command, authority: the expression is harsh, but is not uncommon in the writers of Massinger's time.—GIFFORD.

[5] *Packing,] i. e. insidious contrivance: so the word is used by Shakspeare, and others.*

[6] *Cal. I have all that's requisite*
To the making up of a signior: my spruce ruff,
My hooded cloak, long stocking, and paned hose,
My case of toothpicks, and my silver fork.]
Calandrino is very correct in his enumeration of the articles which in his time made up a complete signior: and which are frequently introduced with evident marks of disapprobation and ridicule by our old poets. The ruff, cloak, and long stocking, are sufficiently familiar: hose are breeches: paned hose are breeches composed of small squares or pannels. Toothpicks, the next accompaniment of state, were newly imported from Italy, as were forks; the want of which our ancestors supplied, as well as they could, with their fingers.—GIFFORD.

[7] *Cal. My grand signior,*
Vouchsafe a beso las manos, &c.]
This is the phrase in which Calandrino supposes his "quondam fellows" will address him. In Massinger's time these tags of politeness were in everybody's mouth, and better understood than they are at this day.—GIFFORD.

ACT IV

SCENE I

The Country. A Hall in Charomonte's House.

Enter **CHAROMONTE** and **LIDIA**.

CHAROMONTE
Daughter, I have observed, since the prince left us,
(Whose absence I mourn with you,) and the visit
Count Sanazarro gave us, you have nourish'd
Sad and retired thoughts, and parted with
That freedom and alacrity of spirit
With which you used to cheer me.

LIDIA
For the count, sir,
All thought of him does with his person die;
But I confess ingenuously, I cannot
So soon forget the choice and chaste delights,
The courteous conversation of the prince,
And without stain, I hope, afforded me,
When he made this house a court.

CHAROMONTE
It is in us
To keep it so without him. Want we know not,
And all we can complain of, Heaven be praised for 't,
Is too much plenty; and we will make use of

[Enter **CAPONI, BERNARDO, PETRUCHIO**, and other **SERVANTS**.

All lawful pleasures.—How now, fellows! when
Shall we have this lusty dance?

CAPONI
In the afternoon, sir.
'Tis a device, I wis, of my own making,
And such a one, as shall make your signiorship know
I have not been your butler for nothing, but

Have crotchets in my head. We'll trip it tightly,
And make my sad young mistress merry again,
Or I'll forswear the cellar.

BERNARDO
If we had
Our fellow Calandrino here, to dance
His part, we were perfect.

PETRUCHIO
O! he was a rare fellow;
But I fear the court hath spoil'd him.

CAPONI
When I was young,
I could have cut a caper on a pinnacle;
But now I am old and wise.—Keep your figure fair,
And follow but the sample I shall set you,
The duke himself will send for us, and laugh at us;
And that were credit.

[Enter **CALANDRINO**.

LIDIA
Who have we here?

CALANDRINO
I find
What was brawn in the country, in the court grows tender.
The bots on these jolting jades! I am bruised to jelly.
A coach for my money!

CHAROMONTE
Calandrino! 'tis he.

CALANDRINO
Now to my postures.—Let my hand have the honour
To convey a kiss from my lips to the cover of
Your foot, dear signior.

CHAROMONTE
Fie! you stoop too low, sir.

CALANDRINO
The hem of your vestment, lady: your glove is for princes;
Nay, I have conn'd my distances.

LIDIA

'Tis most courtly.

CAPONI
Fellow Calandrino!

CALANDRINO
Signior de Caponi,
Grand botelier of the mansion.

BERNARDO
How is 't, man?

[Claps him on the shoulder.

CALANDRINO
Be not so rustic in your salutations.
Signior Bernardo, master of the accounts.
Signior Petruchio, may you long continue
Your function in the chamber!

CAPONI
When shall we learn
Such gambols in our villa?

LIDIA
Sure he's mad.

CHAROMONTE
'Tis not unlike, for most of such mushrooms are so.
What news at court?

CALANDRINO
Basta! they are mysteries.
And not to be reveal'd. With your favour, signior,
I am, in private, to confer awhile
With this signora: but I'll pawn my honour,
That neither my terse language, nor my habit,
Howe'er it may convince, nor my new shrugs,
Shall render her enamour'd.

CHAROMONTE
Take your pleasure;
A little of these apish tricks may pass,
Too much is tedious.

[Exit.

CALANDRINO

The prince, in this paper,
Presents his service. Nay, it is not courtly
To see the seal broke open; so I leave you.—
Signiors of the villa, I'll descend to be
Familiar with you.

CAPONI
Have you forgot to dance?

CALANDRINO
No, I am better'd.

PETRUCHIO
Will you join with us?

CALANDRINO
As I like the project.
Let me warm my brains first with the richest grape,
And then I'm for you.

CAPONI
We will want no wine.

[Exeunt all but **LIDIA**.

LIDIA
That this comes only from the best of princes,
With a kind of adoration does command me
To entertain it; and the sweet contents

[Kissing the letter.

That are inscribed here by his hand must be
Much more than musical to me. All the service
Of my life at no part can deserve this favour.
O, what a virgin longing I feel on me
To unrip the seal, and read it! yet, to break
What he hath fastened, rashly, may appear
A saucy rudeness in me.—I must do it,
(Nor can I else learn his commands, or serve them,)
But with such reverence, as I would open
Some holy writ, whose grave instructions beat down
Rebellious sins, and teach my better part
How to mount upward.—So,

[Opens the letter]

—'tis done, and I

With eagle's eyes will curiously peruse it.

[Reads.

Chaste Lidia, the favours are so great
On me by you conferr'd, that to entreat
The least addition to them, in true sense
May argue me of blushless impudence.
But, such are my extremes, if you deny
A further grace, I must unpitied die.
Haste cuts off circumstance. As you're admired
For beauty; the report of it hath fired
The duke my uncle, and, I fear, you'll prove,
Not with a sacred, but unlawful love.
If he see you as you are, my hoped-for light
Is changed into an everlasting night;
How to prevent it, if your goodness find,
You save two lives, and me you ever bind,
The honourer of your virtues, GIOVANNI.

Were I more deaf than adders, these sweet charms
Would through my ears find passage to my soul,
And soon enchant it. To save such a prince,
Who would not perish? Virtue in him must suffer,
And piety be forgotten. The duke's passion,
Though it raged more than Tarquin's, shall not reach me.
All quaint inventions of chaste virgins aid me!
My prayers are heard; I have 't. The duke ne'er saw me—
Or, if that fail, I am again provided—
But for the servants!—They will take what form
I please to put upon them. Giovanni,
Be safe; thy servant Lidia assures it.
Let mountains of afflictions fall on me,
Their weight is easy, so I set thee free.

[Exit.

SCENE II

Another Room in the Same

Enter **COZIMO, GIOVANNI, SANAZARRO, CHAROMONTE,** and **ATTENDANTS.**

SANAZARRO
Are you not tired with travel, sir?

COZIMO
No, no;
I am fresh and lusty.

CHAROMONTE
This day shall be ever
A holiday to me, that brings my prince
Under my humble roof.

[Weeps.

GIOVANNI
See, sir, my good tutor
Sheds tears for joy.

COZIMO
Dry them up, Charomonte;
And all forbear the room, while we exchange
Some private words together.

GIOVANNI
O, my lord,
How grossly have we overshot ourselves!

SANAZARRO
In what, sir?

GIOVANNI
In forgetting to acquaint
My guardian with our purpose: all that Lidia
Can do avails us nothing, if the duke
Find out the truth from him.

SANAZARRO
'Tis now past help,
And we must stand the hazard:—hope the best, sir.

[Exeunt **GIOVANNI, SANAZARRO**, and **ATTENDANTS**.

CHAROMONTE
My loyalty doubted, sir!

COZIMO
'Tis more. Thou hast
Abused our trust, and in a high degree
Committed treason.

CHAROMONTE

Treason! 'Tis a word
My innocence understands not. Were my breast
Transparent, and my thoughts to be discern'd,
Not one spot shall be found to taint the candour
Of my allegiance: and I must be bold
To tell you, sir, (for he that knows no guilt
Can know no fear,) 'tis tyranny to o'ercharge
An honest man; and such, till now, I've lived,
And such, my lord, I'll die.

COZIMO
Sir, do not flatter
Yourself with hope, these great and glorious words,
Which every guilty wretch, as well as you,
That's arm'd with impudence, can with ease deliver,
And with as full a mouth, can work on us:
Nor shall gay flourishes of language clear
What is in fact apparent.

CHAROMONTE
Fact! what fact?
You, that know only what it is, instruct me,
For I am ignorant.

COZIMO
This, then, sir: We gave up,
On our assurance of your faith and care,
Our nephew Giovanni, nay, our heir
In expectation, to be train'd up by you
As did become a prince.

CHAROMONTE
And I discharged it:
Is this the treason?

COZIMO
Take us with you, sir[1].
And, in respect we knew his youth was prone
To women, and that, living in our court,
He might make some unworthy choice, before
His weaker judgment was confirm'd, we did
Remove him from it; constantly presuming,
You, with your best endeavours, rather would
Have quench'd those heats in him, than light a torch,
As you have done, to his looseness.

CHAROMONTE
I! my travail

Is ill requited, sir; for, by my soul,
I was so curious that way, that I granted
Access to none could tempt him; nor did ever
One syllable, or obscene accent, touch
His ear, that might corrupt him.

COZIMO
No! Why, then,
With your allowance, did you give free way
To all familiar privacy between
My nephew and your daughter? Or why did you
(Had you no other ends in 't but our service)
Read to them, and together, as they had been
Scholars of one form, grammar, rhetoric,
Philosophy, story[2], and interpret to them
The close temptations of lascivious poets?
Or wherefore, for we still had spies upon you,
Was she still present, when, by your advice,
He was taught the use of his weapon, horsemanship,
Nay, wrestling, but to fan a love in her?
And then, forsooth, his exercises ended,
A fair pretence of recreation for him,
(When Lidia was instructed in those graces
That add to beauty,) he, brought to admire her,
Must hear her sing, while to her voice her hand
Made ravishing music; and, this applauded, dance
A light lavolta[3] with her.

CHAROMONTE
Have you ended
All you can charge me with?

COZIMO
Nor stopt you there,
But they must unattended walk into
The silent groves, and hear the amorous birds
Warbling their wanton notes; here, a sure shade
Of barren sicamores, which the all-seeing sun
Could not pierce through; near that, an arbour hung
With spreading eglantine; there, a bubbling spring
Watering a bank of hyacinths and lilies;
With all allurements that could move to love.
And could this, Charomonte, (should I grant
They had been equals both in birth and fortune,)
Become your gravity? nay, 'tis clear as air,
That your ambitious hopes to match your daughter
Into our family, gave connivance to it:
And this, though not in act, in the intent

I call high treason.

CHAROMONTE
Hear my just defence, sir;
And, though you are my prince, it will not take from
Your greatness, to acknowledge with a blush,
In this my accusation you have been
More sway'd by spleen, and jealous suppositions,
Than certain grounds of reason. You had a father,
(Blest be his memory!) that made frequent proofs
Of my loyalty and faith, and, would I boast
The dangers I have broke through in his service,
I could say more. Nay, you yourself, dread sir,
Whenever I was put unto the test,
Found me true gold, and not adulterate metal;
And am I doubted now?

COZIMO
This is from the purpose.

CHAROMONTE
I will come to it, sir: Your grace well knew,
Before the prince's happy presence made
My poor house rich, the chiefest blessing which
I gloried in, though now it prove a curse,
Was an only daughter. Nor did you command me,
As a security to your future fears,
To cast her off: which had you done, howe'er
She was the light of my eyes, and comfort of
My feeble age, so far I prized my duty
Above affection, she now had been
A stranger to my care. But she is fair!
Is that her fault, or mine? Did ever father
Hold beauty in his issue for a blemish?
You may, if you think fit, before my face,
In recompense of all my watchings for you,
With burning corrosives transform her to
An ugly leper. This I will rather suffer, sir,
Than live suspected by you.

COZIMO
Let not passion
Carry you beyond your reason.

CHAROMONTE
I am calm, sir;
Yet you must give me leave to grieve I find
My actions misinterpreted. Alas! sir,

Was Lidia's desire to serve the prince
Call'd an offence? or did she practise to
Seduce his youth, because with her best zeal
And fervour she endeavour'd to attend him?
'Tis a hard construction. Though she be my daughter,
I may thus far speak her: from her infancy
She was ever civil, her behaviour nearer
Simplicity than craft; and malice dares not
Affirm, in one loose gesture, or light language,
She gave a sign she was in thought unchaste.
I'll fetch her to you, sir; and but look on her
With equal eyes, you must in justice grant
That your suspicion wrongs her.

COZIMO
It may be;
But I must have stronger assurance of it
Than passionate words: and, not to trifle time,
As we came unexpected to your house,
We will prevent all means that may prepare her
How to answer that with which we come to charge her.
And howsoever it may be received
As a foul breach to hospitable rites,
On thy allegiance and boasted faith,
Nay, forfeit of thy head, we do confine thee
Close prisoner to thy chamber till all doubts
Are clear'd that do concern us.

CHAROMONTE
I obey, sir,
And wish your grace had followed my hearse
To my sepulchre, my loyalty unsuspected,
Rather than now—But I am silent, sir,
And let that speak my duty[4].

[Exit.

I can't perceive the deficiency

COZIMO
If this man
Be false, disguised treachery ne'er put on
A shape so near to truth. Within, there!

[Re-enter **GIOVANNI** and **SANAZARRO**, ushering in **PETRONELLA**.

[**CALANDRINO** and others setting forth a Banquet.

SANAZARRO
Sir.

COZIMO
Bring Lidia forth.

GIOVANNI
She comes, sir, of herself,
To present her service to you.

COZIMO
Ha! This personage
Cannot invite affection.

SANAZARRO
See you keep state.

PETRONELLA
I warrant you.

COZIMO
The manners of her mind
Must be transcendent, if they can defend
Her rougher outside. May we with your liking
Salute you, lady?

PETRONELLA
Let me wipe my mouth, sir,
With my cambric handkerchief, and then have at you.

COZIMO
Can this be possible?

SANAZARRO
Yes, sir; you will find her
Such as I gave her to you.

PETRONELLA
Will your dukeship
Sit down and eat some sugar-plums? Here's a castle
Of march-pane[5] too; and this quince-marmalade was
Of my own making; all summ'd up together,
Did cost the setting on: and here is wine too,
As good as e'er was tapp'd. I'll be your taster,
For I know the fashion.

[Drinks all off.]

—Now
you must do me right, sir;
You shall nor will nor choose.

GIOVANNI
She's very simple.

COZIMO
Simple! 'tis worse. Do you drink thus often, lady?

PETRONELLA
Still when I am thirsty, and eat when I am hungry:
Such junkets come not every day. Once more to you,
With a heart and a half, i' faith.

COZIMO
Pray you, pause a little.

PETRONELLA
Then I'll drink for you.

COZIMO
I'll find you out a pledge
That shall supply my place: what think you of
This complete signior? You are a Juno,
And in such state must feast this Jupiter:
What think you of him?

PETRONELLA
I desire no better.

COZIMO
And you will undertake this service for me?
You are good at the sport.

CALANDRINO
Who, I? a piddler, sir.

COZIMO
Nay, you shall sit enthroned, and eat and drink
As you were a duke.

CALANDRINO
If your grace will have me,
I'll eat and drink like an emperor.

COZIMO
Take your place, then:

[**CALANDRINO** takes the duke's chair.

We are amazed.

GIOVANNI
This is gross; nor can the imposture
But be discover'd.

SANAZARRO
The duke is too sharp-sighted
To be deluded thus.

CALANDRINO
Nay, pray you eat fair;
Or divide, and I will choose. Cannot you use
Your fork, as I do? Gape, and I will feed you.

[Feeds her.

Gape wider yet; this is courtlike.

PETRONELLA
To choke daws with:—
I like it not.

CALANDRINO
But you like this?

PETRONELLA
Let it come, boy.

[They drink.

COZIMO
What a sight is this! We could be angry with you.
How much you did belie her when you told us
She was only simple! this is barbarous rudeness,
Beyond belief.

GIOVANNI
I would not speak her, sir,
Worse than she was.

SANAZARRO
And I, my lord, chose rather
To deliver her better parted[6] than she is,
Than to take from her.

[Enter **CAPONI,** with his fellow-servants for the dance.

CAPONI
Ere I'll lose my dance,
I'll speak to the purpose. I am, sir, no prologue;
But in plain terms must tell you we are provided
Of a lusty hornpipe.

COZIMO
Prithee let us have it,
For we grow dull.

CAPONI
But to make up the medley,
For it is of several colours, we must borrow
Your grace's ghost here.

CALANDRINO
Pray you, sir, depose me;
It will not do else. I am, sir, the engine

[Rises, and resigns his chair.

By which it moves.

PETRONELLA
I will dance with my duke too;
I will not out.

COZIMO
Begin then.—

[They dance.]

—There's more in this
Than yet I have discover'd. Some Oedipus
Resolve this riddle.

PETRONELLA
Did I not foot it roundly?

[Falls.

COZIMO
As I live, stark drunk! away with her. We'll reward you

[Exeunt **SERVANTS** with **PETRONELLA.**

When you have cool'd yourselves in the cellar.

CAPONI
Heaven preserve you!

COZIMO
We pity Charomonte's wretched fortune
In a daughter, nay, a monster. Good old man!—
The place grows tedious; our remove shall be
With speed: we'll only, in a word or two,
Take leave, and comfort him.

SANAZARRO
'Twill rather, sir,
Increase his sorrow, that you know his shame;
Your grace may do it by letter.

COZIMO
Who sign'd you
A patent to direct us? Wait our coming,
In the garden.

GIOVANNI
All will out.

SANAZARRO
I more than fear it.

[Exeunt **GIOVANNI** and **SANAZARRO**.

COZIMO
These are strange chimeras to us: what to judge of 't,
Is past our apprehension. One command
Charomonte to attend us.

[Exit an **ATTENDANT**.]

Can it be
That Contarino could be so besotted,
As to admire this prodigy! or her father
To dote upon it! Or does she personate,
For some ends unknown to us, this rude behaviour,
Which, in the scene presented, would appear
Ridiculous and impossible?—O, you are welcome.

[Enter **CHAROMONTE**.

We now acknowledge the much wrong we did you
In our unjust suspicion. We have seen
The wonder, sir, your daughter.

CHAROMONTE
And have found her
Such as I did report her. What she wanted
In courtship[7], was, I hope, supplied in civil
And modest entertainment.

COZIMO
Pray you, tell us,
And truly, we command you—Did you never
Observe she was given to drink?

CHAROMONTE
To drink, sir!

COZIMO
Dare you trust your own eyes, if you find her now
More than distemper'd?

CHAROMONTE
I will pull them out, sir,
If your grace can make this good. And if you please
To grant me liberty, as she is I'll fetch her,
And in a moment.

COZIMO
Look you do, and fail not,
On the peril of your head.

CHAROMONTE
Drunk!—She disdains it.

[Exit.

COZIMO
Such contrarieties were never read of.
Charomonte is no fool; nor can I think
His confidence built on sand. We are abused,
'Tis too apparent.

[Re-enter **CHAROMONTE**, with **LIDIA**.

LIDIA
I am indisposed, sir;
And that life you once tender'd, much endanger'd

In forcing me from my chamber.

CHAROMONTE
Here she is, sir;
Suddenly sick, I grant; but sure, not drunk:
Speak to my lord the duke.

LIDIA
All is discover'd.

[Kneels.

COZIMO
Is this your only daughter?

CHAROMONTE
And my heir, sir;
Nor keep I any woman in my house
(Unless for sordid offices) but one
I do maintain, trimm'd up in her cast habits,
To make her sport: and she, indeed, loves wine,
And will take too much of it; and, perhaps, for mirth,
She was presented to you.

COZIMO
It shall yield
No sport to the contrivers. 'Tis too plain now.
Her presence does confirm what Contarino
Deliver'd of her; nor can sickness dim
The splendour of her beauties: being herself, then,
She must exceed his praise.

LIDIA
Will your grace hear me?
I'm faint, and can say little.

COZIMO
Here are accents
Whose every syllable is musical!
Pray you, let me raise you, and awhile rest here.
False Sanazarro, treacherous Giovanni!
But stand we talking!—

CHAROMONTE
Here's a storm soon raised.

COZIMO
As thou art our subject, Charomonte, swear

To act what we command.

CHAROMONTE
That is an oath
I long since took.

COZIMO
Then, by that oath we charge thee,
Without excuse, denial, or delay,
To apprehend, and suddenly, Sanazarro,
And our ingrateful nephew. We have said it.
Do it without reply, or we pronounce thee,
Like them, a traitor to us. See them guarded
In several lodgings, and forbid access
To all, but when we warrant. Is our will
Heard sooner than obey'd?

CHAROMONTE
These are strange turns;
But I must not dispute them.

[Exit.

COZIMO
Be severe in 't.—
O my abused lenity! from what height
Is my power fall'n!

LIDIA
O me most miserable!
That, being innocent, makes others guilty.
Most gracious prince—

COZIMO
Pray you rise, and then speak to me.

LIDIA
My knees shall first be rooted in this earth,
And, Myrrha-like, I'll grow up to a tree,
Dropping perpetual tears of sorrow, which
Harden'd by the rough wind, and turn'd to amber,
Unfortunate virgins like myself shall wear,
Before I'll make petition to your greatness,
But with such reverence, my hands held up thus,
As I would do to heaven. You princes are
As gods on earth to us, and to be sued to
With such humility, as his deputies
May challenge from their vassals.

COZIMO
Here's that form
Of language I expected; pray you, speak:
What is your suit?

LIDIA
That you look upon me
As an humble thing, that millions of degrees
Is placed beneath you: for what am I, dread sir,
Or what can fall in the whole course of my life,
That may be worth your care, much less your trouble?
As the lowly shrub is to the lofty cedar,
Or a molehill to Olympus, if compared,
I am to you, sir. Or, suppose the prince,
(Which cannot find belief in me,) forgetting
The greatness of his birth and hopes, hath thrown
An eye of favour on me, in me punish,
That am the cause, the rashness of his youth.
Shall the queen of the inhabitants of the air,
The eagle, that bears thunder on her wings,
In her angry mood destroy her hopeful young,
For suffering a wren to perch too near them?
Such is our disproportion.

COZIMO
With what fervour
She pleads against herself!

LIDIA
For me, poor maid,
I know the prince to be so far above me,
That my wishes cannot reach him. Yet I am
So much his creature, that, to fix him in
Your wonted grace and favour, I'll abjure
His sight for ever, and betake myself
To a religious life, (where in my prayers
I may remember him,) and ne'er see man more,
But my ghostly father. Will you trust me, sir?
In truth I'll keep my word; or, if this fail,
A little more of fear what may befall him
Will stop my breath for ever.

COZIMO
Had you thus argued

[Raises her.

As you were yourself, and brought as advocates
Your health and beauty to make way for you,
No crime of his could put on such a shape
But I should look with the eyes of mercy on it.
What would I give to see this diamond
In her perfect lustre, as she was before
The clouds of sickness dimm'd it! Yet, take comfort;
And, as you would obtain remission for
His treachery to me, cheer your drooping spirits,
And call the blood again into your cheeks,
And then plead for him; and in such a habit
As in your highest hopes you would put on,
If we were to receive you for our bride.

LIDIA
I'll do my best, sir.

COZIMO
And that best will be
A crown of all felicity to me.

[Exeunt.

FOOTNOTES

[1] Take us with you, sir.]
i. e. understand our meaning fully, before you form your conclusions: this expression is common to all our old writers.

[2] Story,] i. e. history. The two words were formerly synonymous.

[3] Lavolta,] i. e. the waltz. This dance, originally imported from Italy, was a great favourite with our ancestors.

[4] This scene is exquisitely written. It must, however, be confessed, that Charomonte's justification of himself is less complete than might be expected from one who had so good a cause to defend.— GIFFORD.

[5] March-pane,] a cake composed of sugar and almonds.

[6] Parted,] i. e. gifted or endowed with parts.

It seems to have been the opinion of Massinger and his fellow dramatists, that no play could succeed without the admission of some kind of farcical interlude among the graver scenes. If the dramas of our author be intimately considered, few will be found without some extraneous mummery of this description; and, indeed, nothing but a persuasion of the nature which I have just mentioned could give birth to the poor mockery before us. As a trick, it is so gross and palpable, that the duke could not have been deceived by it for a moment; (to do him justice, he frequently hints his suspicions;) and as a piece of humour, it is so low, and even disagreeable, that I cannot avoid regretting a proper regard for his characters had not prevented the author from adopting it on the present occasion.—GIFFORD.

[7] Courtship,] i. e. the grace and elegance of a court.

ACT V

SCENE I

The Same. An Upper Chamber in Charamonte's House.

Enter **SANAZARRO**.

SANAZARRO
'Tis proved in me: the curse of human frailty,
Adding to our afflictions, makes us know
What's good; and yet our violent passions force us
To follow what is ill. Reason assured me
It was not safe to shave a lion's skin;
And that to trifle with a sovereign was
To play with lightning: yet imperious beauty,
Treading upon the neck of understanding,
Compell'd me to put off my natural shape
Of loyal duty, to disguise myself
In the adulterate and cobweb-mask
Of disobedient treachery. Where is now
My borrow'd greatness, or the promised lives
Of following courtiers echoing my will?
In a moment vanish'd! Power that stands not on
Its proper base, which is peculiar only
To absolute princes, falls or rises with
Their frown or favour. The great duke, my master,
(Who almost changed me to his other self,)
No sooner takes his beams of comfort from me,
But I, as one unknown, or unregarded,
Unpitied suffer. Who makes intercession
To his mercy for me now? who does remember
The service I have done him? not a man:
And such as spake no language but my lord
The favourite of Tuscany's grand duke,
Deride my madness.—Ha! what noise of horses?

[He looks out at the back window.

A goodly troop! This back part of my prison

Allows me liberty to see and know them.
Contarino! yes, 'tis he, and Lodovico[1]:
And the duchess Fiorinda, Urbin's heir,
A princess I have slighted: yet I wear
Her favours; and, to teach me what I am,
She whom I scorn'd can only mediate for me.
This way she makes, yet speak to her I dare not;
And how to make suit to her is a task
Of as much difficulty.—Yes, thou blessed pledge

[Takes off the ring.

Of her affection, aid me! This supplies
The want of pen and ink; and this, of paper.

[Takes a pane of glass.

It must be so; and I in my petition
Concise and pithy.

[Exit.

FOOTNOTE

[1] Lodovico,] i. e. Lodovico Hippolito.

SCENE II

The Court Before Charamonte's House.

Enter **CONTARINO**, leading in **FIORINDA, ALPHONSO, HIPPOLITO, HIERONIMO**, and **CALAMINTA**.

FIORINDA
'Tis a goodly pile, this.

HIERONIMO
But better by the owner.

ALPHONSO
But most rich
In the great states[1] it covers.

FIORINDA
The duke's pleasure
Commands us hither.

CONTARINO
Which was laid on us
To attend you to it.

HIPPOLITO
Signior Charomonte,
To see your excellence his guest, will think
Himself most happy.

FIORINDA
Tie my shoe.—

[The pane falls down.]

—What's that?
A pane thrown from the window, no wind stirring!

CALAMINTA
And at your feet too fall'n:—there's something writ on 't.

CONTARINO
Some courtier, belike, would have it known
He wore a diamond.

CALAMINTA
Ha! it is directed
To the princess Fiorinda.

FIORINDA
We will read it.
[Reads.
He, whom you pleased to favour, is cast down
Past hope of rising, by the great duke's frown,
If, by your gracious means, he cannot have
A pardon;—and that got, he lives your slave.
Of men the most distressed,
SANAZARRO.

Of me the most beloved; and I will save thee,
Or perish with thee. Sure, thy fault must be
Of some prodigious shape, if that my prayers
And humble intercession to the duke

[Enter **COZIMO** and **CHAROMONTE**.

Prevail not with him. Here he comes; delay
Shall not make less my benefit.

COZIMO

What we purpose
Shall know no change, and therefore move we not:
We were made as properties, and what we shall
Determine of them cannot be call'd rigour,
But noble justice. When they proved disloyal,
They were cruel to themselves. The prince that pardons
The first affront offer'd to majesty,
Invites a second, rendering that power
Subjects should tremble at, contemptible.
Ingratitude is a monster, Carolo,
To be strangled in the birth, not to be cherish'd.
Madam, you're happily met with.

FIORINDA

Sir, I am
An humble suitor to you; and the rather
Am confident of a grant, in that your grace,
When I made choice to be at your devotion,
Vow'd to deny me nothing.

COZIMO

To this minute
We have confirm'd it. What's your boon?

FIORINDA

It is, sir,
That you, in being gracious to your servant,
The ne'er sufficiently praised Sanazarro,
That now under your heavy displeasure suffers,
Would be good unto yourself. His services,
So many, and so great, (your storm of fury
Calm'd by your better judgment,) must inform you
Some little slip, for sure it is no more,
From his loyal duty, with your justice cannot
Make foul his fair deservings. Great sir, therefore,
Look backward on his former worth, and turning
Your eye from his offence, what 'tis I know not,
And, I am confident, you will receive him
Once more into your favour.

COZIMO

You say well,
You are ignorant in the nature of his fault;
Which when you understand, as we'll instruct you,
Your pity will appear a charity,
It being conferr'd on an unthankful man,

To be repented. He's a traitor, madam,
To you, to us, to gratitude; and in that
All crimes are comprehended.

FIORINDA
If his offence
Aim'd at me only, whatsoe'er it is,
'Tis freely pardon'd.

COZIMO
This compassion in you
Must make the colour of his guilt more ugly.
The honours we have hourly heap'd upon him,
The titles, the rewards, to the envy of
The old nobility, as the common people,
We now forbear to touch at, and will only
Insist on his gross wrongs to you. You were pleased,
Forgetting both yourself and proper greatness,
To favour him, nay, to court him to embrace
A happiness, which, on his knees, with joy
He should have sued for. Who repined not at
The grace you did him? yet, in recompense
Of your large bounties, the disloyal wretch
Makes you a stale; and, what he might be by you,
Scorn'd and derided, gives himself up wholly
To the service of another. If you can
Bear this with patience, we must say you have not
The bitterness of spleen, or ireful passions
Familiar to women. Pause upon it,
And when you seriously have weigh'd his carriage,
Move us again, if your reason will allow it,
His treachery known: and then, if you continue
An advocate for him, we perhaps, because
We would deny you nothing, may awake
Our sleeping mercy. Carolo!

CHAROMONTE
My lord. [They talk aside.

FIORINDA
To endure a rival that were equal to me,
Cannot but speak my poverty of spirit;
But an inferior, more: yet true love must not
Know or degrees, or distances. Lidia may be
As far above me in her form, as she
Is in her birth beneath me; and what I
In Sanazarro liked, he loves in her.
But, if I free him now, the benefit

Being done so timely, and confirming too
My strength and power, my soul's best faculties being
Bent wholly to preserve him, must supply me
With all I am defective in, and bind him
My creature ever. It must needs be so,
Nor will I give it o'er thus.

COZIMO
Does your nephew
Bear his restraint so constantly[2], as you
Deliver it to us?

CHAROMONTE
In my judgment, sir,
He suffers more for his offence to you,
Than in his fear of what can follow it.
For he is so collected, and prepared
To welcome that you shall determine of him,
As if his doubts and fears were equal to him.
And sure he's not acquainted with much guilt,
That more laments the telling one untruth,
Under your pardon still, for 'twas a fault, sir,
Than others, that pretend to conscience, do
Their crying secret sins.

COZIMO
No more; this gloss
Defends not the corruption of the text.
Urge it no more.

[**CHAROMONTE** and the others talk aside.

FIORINDA
I once more must make bold, sir,
To trench upon your patience. I have
Consider'd my wrongs duly: yet that cannot
Divert my intercession for a man
Your grace, like me, once favour'd. I am still
A suppliant to you, that you would vouchsafe
The hearing his defence, and that I may,
With your allowance, see and comfort him.
Then, having heard all that he can allege
In his excuse, for being false to you,
Censure him as you please.

COZIMO
You will o'ercome;
There's no contending with you. Pray you, enjoy

What you desire, and tell him, he shall have
A speedy trial; in which, we will forbear
To sit a judge, because our purpose is
To rise up his accuser.

FIORINDA
All increase
Of happiness wait on Cozimo!

[Exeunt **FIORINDA** and **CALAMINTA**.

ALPHONSO
Was it no more?

CHAROMONTE
My honour's pawn'd for it.

CONTARINO
I'll second you.

HIPPOLITO
Since it is for the service and the safety
Of the hopeful prince, fall what can fall, I'll run
The desperate hazard.

HIERONIMO
He's no friend to virtue
That does decline it.

[They all come forward and kneel.

COZIMO
Ha! what sue you for?
Shall we be ever troubled? Do not tempt
That anger may consume you.

CHAROMONTE
Let it, sir:
The loss is less, though innocents we perish,
Than that your sister's son should fall, unheard,
Under your fury. Shall we fear to entreat
That grace for him, that are your faithful servants,
Which you vouchsafe the count, like us a subject?

COZIMO
Did not we vow, till sickness had forsook
Thy daughter Lidia, and she appear'd
In her perfect health and beauty to plead for him,

We were deaf to all persuasion?

CHAROMONTE
And that hope, sir,
Hath wrought a miracle. She is recover'd,
And, if you please to warrant her, will bring
The penitent prince before you.

COZIMO
To enjoy
Such happiness, what would we not dispense with?

ALPHONSO, HIPPOLITO, HIERONIMO.
We all kneel for the prince.

CONTARINO
Nor can it stand
With your mercy, that are gracious to strangers,
To be cruel to your own.

COZIMO
But art thou certain
I shall behold her at the best?

CHAROMONTE
If ever
She was handsome, as it fits not me to say so,
She is now much better'd.

COZIMO
Rise; thou art but dead,
If this prove otherwise. Lidia, appear,
And feast an appetite almost pined to death
With longing expectation to behold
Thy excellencies: thou, as beauty's queen,
Shalt censure[3] the detractors. Let my nephew
Be led in triumph under her command;
We'll have it so; and Sanazarro tremble
To think whom he hath slander'd. We'll retire
Ourselves a little, and prepare to meet
A blessing, which imagination tells us
We are not worthy of: and then come forth,
But with such reverence, as if I were
Myself the priest, the sacrifice my heart,
To offer at the altar of that goodness
That must or kill or save me.

[Exit.

CHAROMONTE
Are not these
Strange gambols in the duke?

ALPHONSO
Great princes have,
Like meaner men, their weakness.

HIPPOLITO
And may use it
Without control or check.

CONTARINO
'Tis fit they should;
Their privilege were less else, than their subjects'.

HIERONIMO
Let them have their humours; there's no crossing them.

[Exeunt.

FOOTNOTES

[1] States,] i. e. statesmen, men of power. A common acceptation of the word.

[2] So constantly,] i. e. with such constancy.

[3] Censure.] It has been already observed, that this word is used by our old writers, where we should now use judge, and with the same latitude of meaning through its various acceptations.—GIFFORD.

SCENE III

A State-room in the Same.

Enter **FIORINDA, SANAZARRO,** and **CALAMINTA.**

SANAZARRO
And can it be, your bounties should fall down
In showers on my ingratitude, or the wrongs
Your greatness should revenge, teach you to pity?
What retribution can I make, what service
Pay to your goodness, that, in some proportion,
May to the world express I would be thankful?
Since my engagements are so great, that all

My best endeavours to appear your creature
Can but proclaim my wants, and what I owe
To your magnificence.

FIORINDA
All debts are discharged
In this acknowledgment: yet, since you please
I shall impose some terms of satisfaction
For that which you profess yourself obliged for,
They shall be gentle ones, and such as will not,
I hope, afflict you.

SANAZARRO
Make me understand,
Great princess, what they are, and my obedience
Shall, with all cheerful willingness, subscribe
To what you shall command.

FIORINDA
I will bind you to
Make good your promise. First, I then enjoin you
To love a lady, that, a noble way,
Truly affects you; and that you would take
To your protection and care the dukedom
Of Urbin, which no more is mine, but yours.
And that, when you have full possession of
My person as my fortune, you would use me,
Not as a princess, but instruct me in
The duties of an humble wife, for such,
The privilege of my birth no more remember'd,
I will be to you. This consented to,
All injuries are forgotten.

SANAZARRO
I am wretched,
In having but one life to be employ'd
As you please to dispose it. And, believe it,
If it be not already forfeited
To the fury of my prince, as 'tis your gift,
With all the faculties of my soul I'll study,
In what I may, to serve you.

FIORINDA
I am happy

[Enter **GIOVANNI** and **LIDIA**.

In this assurance. What sweet lady's this?

SANAZARRO
'Tis Lidia, madam, she—

FIORINDA
I understand you.
Nay, blush not; by my life, she is a rare one!
And, if I were your judge, I would not blame you
To like and love her. But, sir, you are mine now;
And I presume so on your constancy,
That I dare not be jealous.

SANAZARRO
All thoughts of her
Are in your goodness buried.

LIDIA
Pray you, sir,
Be comforted; your innocence should not know
What 'tis to fear; and if that you but look on
The guards that you have in yourself, you cannot.
The duke's your uncle, sir, and, though a little
Incensed against you, when he sees your sorrow,
He must be reconciled. What rugged Tartar,
Or cannibal, though bathed in human gore,
But, looking on your sweetness, would forget
His cruel nature, and let fall his weapon,
Though then aim'd at your throat?

GIOVANNI
O Lidia,
Of maids the honour, and your sex's glory!
It is not fear to die, but to lose you,
That brings this fever on me. I will now
Discover to you, that which, till this minute,
I durst not trust the air with. Ere you knew
What power the magic of your beauty had,
I was enchanted by it, liked, and loved it,
My fondness still increasing with my years;
And, flatter'd by false hopes, I did attend
Some blessed opportunity to move
The duke with his consent to make you mine:
But now, such is my star-cross'd destiny,
When he beholds you as you are, I may
As well entreat him give away his crown,
As to part from a jewel of more value.
Yet, howsoever, when you are his duchess,
And I am turn'd into forgotten dust,

Pray you, love my memory:—I should say more,
But I'm cut off.

[Enter **COZIMO, CHAROMONTE, CONTARINO, HIERONIMO, HIPPOLITO**, and **ALPHONSO**.

SANAZARRO
The duke! That countenance, once,
When it was clothed in smiles, show'd like an angel's,
But, now 'tis folded up in clouds of fury,
'Tis terrible to look on.

LIDIA
Sir.

COZIMO
A while
Silence your musical tongue, and let me feast
My eyes with the most ravishing object that
They ever gazed on. There's no miniature
In her fair face, but is a copious theme
Which would, discoursed at large of, make a volume.
What clear arch'd brows! what sparkling eyes! the lilies
Contending with the roses in her cheeks,
Who shall most set them off. What ruby lips!—
Or unto what can I compare her neck,
But to a rock of crystal? every limb
Proportion'd to love's wish, and in their neatness
Add lustre to the riches of her habit,
Not borrow from it.

LIDIA
You are pleased to show, sir,
The fluency of your language, in advancing
A subject much unworthy.

COZIMO
How! unworthy?
By all the vows which lovers offer at
The Cyprian goddess' altars, eloquence
Itself presuming, as you are, to speak you,
Would be struck dumb!—And what have you deserved then,

[**GIOVANNI** and **SANAZARRO** kneel.

Wretches, you kneel too late, that have endeavour'd
To spout the poison of your black detraction
On this immaculate whiteness? Was it malice
To her perfections? or—

FIORINDA
Your highness promised
A gracious hearing to the count.

LIDIA
And prince too:
Do not make void so just a grant.

COZIMO
We will not:
Yet, since their accusation must be urged,
And strongly, ere their weak defence have hearing,
We seat you here, as judges, to determine
Of your gross wrongs and ours.

[Seats the **LADIES** in the chairs of state.]

And now, remembering
Whose deputies you are, be neither sway'd
Or with particular spleen, or foolish pity,
For neither can become you.

CHAROMONTE
There's some hope yet,
Since they have such gentle judges.

COZIMO
Rise, and stand forth, then,
And hear, with horror to your guilty souls,
What we will prove against you. Could this princess,
Thou enemy to thyself, [To **SANAZARRO**] stoop her high flight
Of towering greatness to invite thy lowness
To look up to it, and with nimble wings
Of gratitude couldst thou forbear to meet it?
Were her favours boundless in a noble way,
And warranted by our allowance, yet,
In thy acceptation, there appear'd no sign
Of a modest thankfulness?

FIORINDA
Pray you, forbear
To press that further; 'tis a fault we have
Already heard, and pardon'd.

COZIMO
We will then
Pass over it, and briefly touch at that

Which does concern ourself; in which both being
Equal offenders, what we shall speak points
Indifferently at either. How we raised thee,
Forgetful Sanazarro! of our grace,
To a full possession of power and honours,
It being too well known, we'll not remember.
And what thou wert, rash youth, in expectation,
[To **GIOVANNI**]
And from which headlong thou hast thrown thyself,
Not Florence, but all Tuscany, can witness
With admiration. To assure thy hopes,
We did keep constant to a widow'd bed,
And did deny ourself those lawful pleasures
Our absolute power and height of blood allow'd us;
Made both, the keys that open'd our heart's secrets,
And what you spake, believed as oracles:
But you, in recompense of this, to him
That gave you all, to whom you owed your being,
With treacherous lies endeavour'd to conceal
This jewel from our knowledge, which ourself
Could only lay just claim to.

GIOVANNI
'Tis most true, sir.

SANAZARRO
We both confess a guilty cause.

COZIMO
Look on her.
Is this a beauty fit to be embraced
By any subject's arms? can any tire
Become that forehead but a diadem?
Or, should we grant your being false to us
Could be excused, your treachery to her,
In seeking to deprive her of that greatness
(Her matchless worth consider'd) she was born to,
Must ne'er find pardon. We have spoken, ladies,
Like a rough orator, that brings more truth
Than rhetoric to make good his accusation;
And now expect your sentence.

[The **LADIES** descend from the state[1].

LIDIA
In your birth, sir,
You were mark'd out the judge of life and death,
And we, that are your subjects, to attend,

With trembling fear, your doom.

FIORINDA
We do resign
This chair, as only proper to yourself.

GIOVANNI
And, since injustice we are lost, we fly
Unto your saving mercy.

[All kneeling.

SANAZARRO
Which sets off
A prince much more than rigour.

CHAROMONTE
And becomes him,
When 'tis express'd to such as fell by weakness,
That being a twin-born brother to affection,
Better than wreaths of conquest.

HIERONIMO, HIPPOLITO, CONTARINO, ALPHONSO.
We all speak
Their language, mighty sir.

COZIMO
You know our temper,
And therefore with more boldness venture on it:
And, would not our consent to your demands
Deprive us of a happiness hereafter
Ever to be despair'd of, we, perhaps,
Might hearken nearer to you; and could wish
With some qualification, or excuse,
You might make less the mountains of your crimes,
And so invite our clemency to feast with you.
But you, that knew with what impatiency
Of grief we parted from the fair Clarinda,
Our duchess, (let her memory still be sacred!)
And with what imprecations on ourself
We vow'd, not hoping e'er to see her equal,
Ne'er to make trial of a second choice,
If nature framed not one that did excel her,
As this maid's beauty prompts us that she does:—
And yet, with oaths then mix'd with tears, upon
Her monument we swore our eye should never
Again be tempted;—'tis true, and those vows
Are register'd above, something here tells me.—

Carolo, thou heard'st us swear.

CHAROMONTE
And swear so deeply,
That if all women's beauties were in this,
(As she's not to be named with the dead duchess,)
Nay, all their virtues bound up in one story,
(Of which mine is scarce an epitome,)
If you should take her as a wife, the weight
Of your perjuries would sink you. If I durst,
I had told you this before.

COZIMO
'Tis strong truth, Carolo:
And yet what was necessity in us
Cannot free them from treason.

CHAROMONTE
There's your error:
The prince, in care to have you keep your vows
Made unto Heaven, vouchsafed to love my daughter[2].

LIDIA
He told me so, indeed, sir.

FIORINDA
And the count
Averr'd as much to me.

COZIMO
You all conspire,
To force our mercy from us.

CHAROMONTE
Which given up,
To aftertimes preserves you unforsworn:
An honour which will live upon your tomb
When your greatness is forgotten.

COZIMO
Though we know
All this is practice[3], and that both are false,
Such reverence we will pay to dead Clarinda,
And to our serious oaths, that we are pleased
With our own hand to blind our eyes, and not
Know what we understand. Here, Giovanni,
We pardon thee; and take from us, in this,
More than our dukedom: love her. As I part

With her, all thoughts of women fly fast from us.
Sanazarro, we forgive you: in your service
To this princess, merit it. Yet let not others
That are in trust and grace, as you have been,
By the example of our lenity,
Presume upon their sovereign's clemency.

[Enter **CALANDRINO** and **PETRONELLA**.

OMNES
Long live great Cozimo!

CALANDRINO
Sure the duke is
In the giving vein, they are so loud. Come on, spouse;
We have heard all, and we will have our boon too.

COZIMO
What is it?

CALANDRINO
That your grace, in remembrance of
My share in a dance, and that I play'd your part
When you should have drunk hard, would get this signior's grant
To give this damsel to me in the church,
For we are contracted. In it you shall do
Your dukedom pleasure.

COZIMO
How?

CALANDRINO
Why, the whole race
Of such as can act naturally fools' parts
Are quite worn out; and they that do survive
Do only zany us: and we will bring you,
If we die not without issue, of both sexes
Such chopping mirth-makers, as shall preserve
Perpetual cause of sport, both to your grace
And your posterity, that sad melancholy
Shall ne'er approach you.

COZIMO
We are pleased in it,
And will pay her portion.—

[Comes forward.

May the passage prove,
Of what's presented, worthy of your love
And favour, as was aim'd; and we have all
That can in compass of our wishes fall.

[Exeunt.

FOOTNOTES

[1] The state,] i. e. the raised platform on which the chairs were placed.

[2] The prince, in care to have you keep your vows
Made unto Heaven, vouchsafed to love my daughter.]
This attempt to impose upon the great duke is more deplorable than the former. It has falsehood and improbability written on its face. The duke, indeed, is not deceived by it; but surely the author showed a strange want of judgment in this gratuitous degradation of three of his most —estimable characters.— GIFFORD.

Surely Massinger intended that his characters should here be understood as speaking the truth. The contrivance by which he exculpates Giovanni is a clumsy one; but he was anxious to conclude his play, and took the first that suggested itself. Awkward as it may appear to the reader, it has, perhaps, quite enough dramatic probability to satisfy an audience

[3] Practice,] i. e. artifice, or insidious combination.

PHILIP MASSINGER — A SHORT BIOGRAPHY

Very few materials exist for a life of Massinger beyond the entries of the Parish Register or the College Books, and a few slender intimations scattered here and there in the dedications to his plays. From these scanty sources the following brief memoir is derived.

Our author was born at Salisbury[1] in the year 1584: he was the son of Arthur Massinger, a gentleman in the service of Henry, the second Earl of Pembroke[2]. We must not suppose, from his being thus attached to the family of a nobleman, that the father of our poet was a person of inferior birth and station. In those days the word servant carried with it no sense of degradation. The great lords and officers of the court numbered inferior nobles among their followers. We read, in Cavendish's Life of Wolsey, that "my Lord Percy, the son and heir of the Earl of Northumberland, attended upon and was servitor to the lord-cardinal[3]:" and from the situation which Arthur Massinger held in the household of so high and influential a person as the Earl of Pembroke, we might be justly led to argue rather favourably than unfavourably of his family and his connexions. "There were," says Mr. Gifford, "many considerations which united to render this state of dependance respectable and even honourable. The secretaries, clerks, and assistants, of various departments, were not then, as now, nominated by the government, but left to the choice of the person who held the employment; and as no particular dwelling was officially set apart for their residence, they were entertained in the house of their principal. That communication, too, between noblemen of power and trust, both of a public and private nature, which is now committed to the post, was in those days managed by confidential servants, who were despatched from one to the other, and even to the sovereign[4];" and, indeed, the father of our poet himself was, we know, in one instance thus employed as the bearer of communications from his patron to Elizabeth. We read in The Sidney Letters[5], "Mr. Massinger is newly come up from the Earl of Pembroke with letters to the queen for his lordship's leave to be away this St. George's Day." This was an errand which would not have been intrusted to the execution of any inconsiderable person: unimportant as the occasion may appear to us, it would not have been regarded in that light by Elizabeth; for no monarch ever exacted from the nobility, and particularly from her officers of state, a more rigid and scrupulous compliance with stated order than this princess.

With regard to the early youth of Massinger, we possess no information whatever. Mr. Gifford supposes that it might have been passed at Wilton, a seat belonging to the Earl of Pembroke, in the neighbourhood of Salisbury; but this mode of disposing of his early years rests on a very improbable conjecture. It may occasionally have happened that the child of a favourite dependant was admitted as the companion of the younger branches of the patron's family, and allowed to receive his education among them; but this was certainly not an ordinary case; and, like Cavendish, a large majority of the great man's servants and dependants "left wife and children, home and family, rest and quietness, only to serve him[6]."—Massinger was most likely educated at the grammar-school of Salisbury, where many distinguished characters have received the rudiments of their education, among whom the elegant and accomplished Addison is to be numbered. But wherever the first years of our poet's life may have been spent, and whatever may have been the nature of his education, we know that at the age of eighteen (May 14, 1602) he was entered at the university of Oxford, and became a commoner of St. Alban's Hall[7].

Massinger resided at Oxford about four years, and then abruptly left it, without taking any degree. The cause of this sudden departure is ascribed by Mr. Gifford to the death of his father, from whom his supplies were derived: but Davies relates a very different story, and asserts that the Earl of Pembroke, who had sent him to the university and maintained him there, withdrew the necessary allowance in consequence of his having misapplied the time demanded for severer studies, in the pursuit of a more attractive but less profitable description of literature. Each opinion is equally ungrounded on the basis of any substantial evidence, and rests almost entirely on the imagination of the biographer: what slight authority there is favours the latter supposition, which, perhaps, on the whole, is most consistent with the known circumstances of the case. Anthony Wood, who was born, lived, and died at Oxford; who spent his time in collecting and recording the gossip which circulated in the university respecting the characters and conduct of its more distinguished sons; and whose evidence, however indifferent it may be, is the best that can be obtained upon the subject, confirms the representation of Davies:— "Massinger," says Wood, "gave his mind more to poetry and romance, for about four years or more, than to logic and philosophy, which he ought to have done, as he was patronised to that end." This passage corroborates the account of Davies so far as to intimate that patronage was afforded to our author, and that cause of dissatisfaction was given to the patron; but it goes no farther: it does not even state to whom the poet was indebted for assistance, nor that the misapplication of his academic hours was at all resented by the friend from whom the assistance was received: but still Wood is very probably correct in his information that other than his paternal funds were depended upon for maintaining Massinger at the university; and if such was the case, there can be no question from whose hands they must have proceeded; while the simple fact of his having been totally neglected, from the time of his father's death, by the whole of the Pembroke family, till after the demise of the earl, carries with it a strong suspicion that some offence was committed on the side of the poet, and tenaciously remembered on the side of the peer. Henry, the second Earl of Pembroke, died (1601) the year before

Massinger was admitted at Oxford; and William, the third earl, to whom the father of Massinger continued attached during life, is universally and justly considered one of the brightest ornaments of the courts of Elizabeth and James. He was a man of generous and liberal disposition; the distinguished patron of arts and learning; and a lover of poetry, which he himself cultivated with some degree of success. It is not probable—it is impossible—that such a man should have allowed the highly talented son of an old and faithful servant of his family to be checked in his course of study, and abandoned to maintain, through the early years of life, a single-handed contest with adversity, for the want of that pecuniary aid which he could have yielded and never missed, unless some strong and decided cause of displeasure had existed. Had Massinger been merely forced to leave the university, as Mr. Gifford supposes, because the funds necessary to maintain him there had failed with the life of his father, we impute an act of illiberality to the Earl of Pembroke which is inconsistent with the whole tenor of his life and character. From whatever source the expenses of our author's education were originally defrayed, their suddenly ceasing argues in favour of the account intimated by Wood and detailed by Davies. If his father had, during his life, supported him at the university, there must have been some reason for the earl's not continuing that support when the father of Massinger was no more; and perhaps the most honourable supposition for both parties is that which represents the earl as offended by the bent of our author's studies and pursuits. By adopting this view of the case we are saved from the painful necessity of either assuming, on the one hand, that a nobleman distinguished among the most amiable characters of his age allowed a highly gifted and meritorious young man, a natural dependant of his house, to languish in the want of that countenance and protection on which he had an hereditary claim; or, on the other hand, that Massinger had incurred the displeasure of his natural and hereditary patron by the commission of some more crying offence.

Every, even the slightest, surmise of Mr. Gifford is deserving attention and respect; but I cannot admit the supposition by which he would account for the alienation that subsisted between the Earl of Pembroke and our author. That distinguished critic has inferred, from the religious sentiments contained in The Virgin Martyr, that Massinger was a Roman catholic, and for that cause neglected by the protector of his father. But if the intimations scattered through this play and others should be received as sufficient evidence of the faith of Massinger, we must, on similar evidence—the intimations contained in Measure for Measure, for instance—conclude that the religion of Shakspeare was the same; and then we are cast back upon our old difficulty, and have to explain why William Earl of Pembroke, a celebrated patron of literary men, and of dramatists in particular, scorned to yield his notice to the catholic Massinger, while (to use the expression of Heminge and Condell) he "prosequuted" the catholic Shakspeare and "his works with so much favour[8]?" There are many reasons for believing Shakspeare to have been a member of the church of Rome; and the patronage afforded him by the Earl of Pembroke proves, that that nobleman extended his liberality to men of genius without any regard to distinctions of faith; but, on the other hand, we have no just grounds for assuming that Massinger really did hold the same opinions. The only evidence we have upon this point, that afforded by the general tone of his writings, is of a most vague and superficial description. What, in fact, can be inferred from it? We may from such a source derive very satisfactory information respecting the sentiments which would be favourably received by the audience, but very little respecting those of the author. The truth is, that though the national religion was reformed in its liturgy and articles, the feelings, prejudices, and superstitions of the people were still almost entirely catholic; and Massinger, like any other dramatic author, writing for the amusement of the people, necessarily addressed them in a language they would understand, and with sentiments that accorded with their own. Besides, as a poet, he would never carry his theological distinctions to his literary labours: Voltaire himself is catholic in his tragedies; and Massinger naturally adopted the creed which was most suitable to the purposes of poetry, and afforded the most picturesque ceremonies and romantic situations. I feel inclined, therefore, to dismiss entirely the theory suggested by Mr. Gifford, for these two reasons; first, supposing our author to have been a catholic, we have no reason for condemning the Earl of Pembroke as a bigot and a persecutor, who would close his eyes to the merits of so great an author, because his faith did not tally with his own; and, secondly, we have no sufficient grounds for supposing him to have been a catholic at all. But with regard to all such visionary conjectures, thinking is literally a waste of thought.

Whatever may have been the nature of Massinger's studies at Oxford, it is quite certain, from the general character of his works, that his time could not have been wasted there; and his literary acquirements, at the period of his leaving the university, appear to have been multifarious and extensive. He was about two-and-twenty (1606) when he arrived in London, where, as he more than once observes, he was driven by his necessities, and somewhat inclined, perhaps, by the peculiar bent of his talents, to dedicate himself to the service of the stage.

The theatre, when Massinger first took up his abode in the metropolis, must have presented attractions of all others the most calculated to excite the interest, and inspire the imagination, of a young man of sensibility, taste, and education like our poet. No art ever attained a more rapid maturity than the dramatic art in England. The people had, indeed, been long accustomed to a species of exhibition, called MIRACLES or MYSTERIES, founded on sacred subjects, and performed by the ministers of religion themselves, on the holy festivals, in or near the churches, and designed to instruct the ignorant in the leading facts of sacred history[9]. From the occasional introduction of allegorical characters, such as Faith, Death, Hope, or Sin, into these religious dramas, representations of another kind, called MORALITIES, had by degrees arisen, of which the plots were more artificial, regular, and connected, and which were entirely formed of such personifications: but the first rough draught of a regular tragedy and comedy—Lord Sackville's Gorboduc, and Still's Gammer Gurton's Needle[10]—were not produced till within the latter half of the sixteenth century, and little more than twenty years before the stage acquired its highest splendour in the productions of Shakspeare.

About the end of the sixteenth century, the attention of the public began to be more generally directed to the drama; and it throve most admirably beneath the cheering beams of popular favour. The theatrical performances which in the early part of Elizabeth's reign had been exhibited on temporary stages, erected in such halls or apartments as the actors could procure, or, more generally, in the yards of the larger inns, while the spectators surveyed them from the surrounding windows and galleries, began to find more convenient and permanent habitations. About the year 1569, a regular playhouse, under the appropriate name of The Theatre, was erected. It is supposed to have stood somewhere in Blackfriars; and, three years after the commencement of this establishment, the queen, yielding to her own inclination for such amusements, and disregarding the remonstrances of the Puritans, granted licence and authority to the servants of the Earl of Leicester ("for the recreation of her loving subjects, as for her own solace and pleasure when she should think good to see them") to exercise their occupation throughout the whole realm of England. From this time the number of theatres increased with the increasing demands of the people. Various noblemen had their respective companies of performers, who were associated as their servants, and acted under their protection; and when Massinger left Oxford, and commenced dramatic author, there were no less than seven principal theatres open in the metropolis.

With respect to the interior arrangements, there were very few points of difference between our modern theatres and those of the days of Massinger. The prices of admission, indeed, were considerably cheaper: to the boxes the entrance was a shilling; to the pit and galleries only sixpence. Sixpence also was the price paid for stools upon the stage; and these seats, as we learn from Decker's Gull's Hornbook, were particularly affected by the wits and critics of the time. The conduct of the audience was less restrained by the sense of public decorum, and smoking tobacco, playing at cards, eating and drinking, were generally prevalent among them. The hours of performance were also earlier: the play commencing at one o'clock. During the representation a flag was unfurled at the top of the theatre; and the stage, according to the universal practice of the age, was strewn with rushes; but, in all other respects, the theatres of Elizabeth and James's days seem to have borne a perfect resemblance to our own. They had their pit, where the inferior class of spectators, the groundlings, vented their clamorous censure or approbation; they had their boxes—rooms as they were called—to which the right of exclusive admission was engaged by the night, for the more affluent portion of the audience; and there were again the galleries, or scaffoldings above the boxes, for those who were content to purchase less commodious situations at a cheaper rate. On the stage, in the same manner, the appointments appear to have been nearly of the same description as at present. The curtain divided the audience from the actors, which, at the third sounding, not indeed of the bell, but of the trumpet, was drawn for the commencement of the performance. Malone, in his account of the ancient theatre, supposes that there were no moveable scenes; that a permanent elevation of about nine feet was raised at the back of the stage, from which, in many of the old plays, part of the dialogue was spoken; and that there was a private box on each side this platform. Such an arrangement would have destroyed all theatrical illusion; and it seems extraordinary that any spectators should desire to fix themselves in a station where they could have seen nothing but the backs and trains of the performers; but, as Malone himself acknowledges the spot to have been inconvenient, and that "it is not very easy to ascertain the precise situation where these boxes really were[11]", it may very reasonably be presumed, that they were not placed in the position that the historian of the English stage has supposed. As to the permanent floor, or upper stage, of which he speaks, he may or may not be correct in his statement. All that his quotations upon the subject really establish is, that in the old, as in the modern theatre, when the actor was to speak from a window, or balcony, or the walls of a fortress, the requisite ingenuity was not wanting to contrive a representation of the place. But with regard to the use of painted moveable scenery, it is not possible, from the very circumstances of the case, to believe him correct in his theory. Such a contrivance could not have escaped our ancestors. All the materials were ready to their hands. They had not to invent for themselves, but merely to adapt an old invention to that peculiar purpose; and at a time when every better-furnished apartment was adorned with tapestry; when even the rooms of the commonest taverns were hung with painted cloths; while all the materials were constantly before their eyes, we can hardly believe our forefathers to have been so deficient in ingenuity, as to have missed the simple contrivance of converting the common ornaments of their walls into the decorations of their theatres. But, in fact, the use of scenery was almost co-existent with the introduction of dramatic representations in this country. In the Chester Mysteries (1268), the most ancient and complete collection of the kind which we possess, is found the following stage direction: "Then Noe shall go into the arke with all his familye, his wife excepte. The arke must be boarded round about; and upon the boardes all the beastes and fowles, hereafter rehearsed, must be painted, that their wordes may agree with their pictures[12]." In this passage we have a clear reference to a painted scene. It is not likely that, in the lapse of three centuries, while all other arts were in a state of rapid improvement, and the art of dramatic writing, perhaps, more rapidly and successfully improved than any other, the art of theatrical decoration should have alone stood still. It is not improbable that their scenes were few; and that they were varied, as occasion might require, by the introduction of different pieces of stage furniture. Mr. Gifford, who adheres to the opinions of Malone, says, "A table with a pen and ink thrust in, signified that the stage was a counting-house; if these were withdrawn and two stools put in their place, it was then a tavern[13]." And this might be perfectly satisfactory as long as the business of the play was supposed to be passing within doors; but when it was removed to the open air, such meagre devices would no longer be sufficient to guide the imagination of the audience, and some new method must have been adopted to indicate the place of action. After giving the subject very considerable attention, I cannot help thinking that Steevens was right in rejecting Malone's theory, and concluding that the spectators were, as at the present day, assisted in following the progress of the story by means of painted moveable scenery. This opinion is confirmed by the ancient stage directions. In the folio Shakspeare, 1623, we read "Enter Brutus in his orchard; Enter Timon in the woods; Enter Timon from the cave." In Coriolanus, "Marcius follows them to the gates and is shut in." Innumerable instances of the same kind might be cited to prove that the ancient stage was not so defective in the necessary decorations as some antiquaries of great authority would represent. "It may be added," says Steevens, "that the dialogue of our old dramatists has such perpetual reference to objects supposed visible to the audience, that the want of scenery could not have failed to render many of the descriptions absurd. Banquo examines the outside of Inverness castle with such minuteness, that he distinguishes even the nests which the martens had built under the projecting part of its roof. Romeo, standing in a garden, points to the tops of fruit-trees gilded by the moon. The prologue speaker to the second part of Henry the Fourth expressly shows the spectators 'This worm-eaten hold of ragged stone,' in which Northumberland was lodged. Iachimo takes the most exact inventory of every article in Imogen's bed-chamber, from the silk and silver of which her tapestry was wrought, down to the Cupids that support her andirons. Had not the inside of the apartment, with its proper furniture, been represented, how ridiculous must the action of Iachimo have appeared! He must have stood looking out of the room for the particulars supposed to be visible within it." The works of Massinger would afford innumerable instances of a similar kind to vindicate the opinion which Steevens has asserted on the testimony of Shakspeare alone. But on this subject there is one passage which appears to me quite conclusive. Must not all the humour of the mock play in The Midsummer Night's Dream have been entirely lost, unless the audience before whom it was performed were accustomed to all the embellishments requisite to give effect to a dramatic representation, and could consequently estimate the absurdity of those shallow contrivances and mean substitutes for scenery devised by the ignorance of the clowns[14]?

In only one respect do I perceive any material difference between the mode of representation at the time of Massinger and at present: in his day, the female parts were performed by boys. This custom, which must in many cases have materially injured the illusion of the scene, was in others of considerable advantage: it furnished the stage with a succession of youths, regularly educated for the art, to fill, in every department of the drama, the characters suited to their age. When the lad had become too tall for Juliet, he had acquired the skill, and was most admirably fitted, both in age and appearance, for performing the part which Garrick considered the most difficult on the stage, because it needed "an old head upon young shoulders," the ardent and arduous character of Romeo. When the voice had "the mannish crack," that rendered the youth unfit to appear as the representative of the gentle Imogen, the stage possessed in him the very person that was wanting to do justice to the princely sentiments of Arviragus or Guiderius[15].

Such was the state of the stage when Massinger arrived in the metropolis, and dedicated his talents to its service. He joined a splendid fraternity, for Shakspeare, Jonson, Beaumont, Fletcher, Shirley, were then flourishing at the height of their reputation, and the full vigour of their genius. Massinger came among them no unworthy competitor for such honours and emoluments as the theatre could afford. Of the honours, indeed, he seems to have reaped a very fair and equitable portion; of the emoluments, the harvest was less abundant. In those days, very little pecuniary reward was to be gained by the dramatic poet, unless, as indeed was most frequently the case, he added the profession of the actor to that of the author, and recited the verses which he wrote. The distinguished performers of that time, Alleyn, Burbage, Heminge, Condell, Shakspeare, all appear to have died in independent, if not affluent, circumstances; but the remuneration obtained by the poet was most miserably curtailed. The price given at the theatre for a new play fluctuated between ten and twenty pounds; the copyright, if the piece was printed, might produce from six to ten pounds more; in addition to these sums, the dedication-fee may be reckoned, the usual amount of which was forty shillings. Our author appears to have produced about two or three plays every year. Most of them were successful; but, even with this industry and good fortune, his annual income would rarely have exceeded fifty pounds: and we cannot, therefore, feel surprised at finding him continually speaking of his necessities; or that the only existing document connected with his life should be one that represents him in a state of pecuniary embarrassment.

Among the papers of Dulwich College, the indefatigable Mr. Malone discovered the following letter tripartite, which, coming from persons of such deserved celebrity, cannot fail of interesting the reader.

"To our most loving friend, Mr. Phillip Hinchlow, esquire, these.

"Mr. Hinchlow,

"You understand our unfortunate extremitie, and I doe not thincke you so void of Christianitie but that you would throw so much money into the Thames as wee request now of you, rather than endanger so many innocent lives. You know there is xl. more, at least, to be receaved of you for the play. We desire you to lend us vl. of that, which shall be allowed to you; without which, we cannot be bayled, nor I play any more till this be dispatch'd. It will lose you xxl. ere the end of the next weeke, besides the hindrance of the next new play. Pray, sir, consider our cases with humanity, and now give us cause to acknowledge you our true freind in time of neede. Wee have entreated Mr. Davison to deliver this note, as well to witness your love as our promises, and alwayes acknowledgement to be ever

"Your most thankfull and loving friends,
"NAT. FIELD[16]."

"The money shall be abated out of the money remayns for the play of Mr. Fletcher and ours.
"ROB. DABORNE[17]."

"I have ever found you a true loving friend to mee, and in soe small a suite, it beinge honest, I hope you will not fail us.
"PHILIP MASSINGER."

Indorsed.
"Received by mee, Robert Davison, of Mr. Hinchlow, for the use of Mr. Daboerne, Mr. Feeld, Mr. Messenger, the sum of vl.
"ROB. DAVISON[18]."

The occasion of the distress in which these three distinguished persons were involved it is not possible to fathom. We may imagine a thousand emergencies, either creditable or discreditable to the fame of the writers, with which the letter would perfectly tally; but, on such slight and vague intimations, no ingenuity could determine which was most likely to be correct. But from the document a circumstance is ascertained, which, before its discovery, had been called in question. Sir Aston Cockayne, a friend of Massinger, had asserted in a volume of poems, published in 1658, that our author had written in conjunction with Fletcher; Davies doubted this report, but the above letter establishes the fact beyond the possibility of dispute.

Massinger is known to have produced thirty-seven plays for the stage, a list of which is given at the conclusion of this memoir. Sixteen entire plays and the fragment of another, The Parliament of Love, alone are extant. No less than eleven of his productions, in manuscript, were in possession of Mr. Warburton (Somerset Herald), and destroyed with the rest of that gentleman's invaluable collection by his cook, who, ignorant of their worth, used them as waste paper for the purposes of the kitchen.

The great and various merits of the works of Massinger will be better seen in the following volumes than in any elaborate, critical dissertation. If our author be compared with the other dramatic writers of his age, we cannot long hesitate where to place him. More natural in his characters and more poetical in his diction than Jonson or Cartwright, more elevated and nervous than Fletcher, the only writers who can be supposed to contest his pre-eminence, Massinger ranks immediately under Shakspeare himself. Our poet excels, perhaps, more in the description than in the expression of passion; this may in some measure be ascribed to his attention to the fable: while his scenes are managed with consummate skill, the lighter shades of character and sentiment are lost in the tendency of each part to the catastrophe. The melody, force, and variety of his versification are always remarkable. The prevailing beauties of his productions are dignity and elegance; their predominant fault is want of passion.

Massinger's last play—which is unfortunately lost—The Anchoress of Pausilippo, was acted Jan. 26, 1640, about six weeks before his death, which happened on the 17th of March, 1640. He went to bed in good health, says Langbaine, and was found dead in the morning, in his own house on the Bankside. He was buried in the churchyard of St. Saviour's, and the comedians paid the last sad duty to his name, by attending him to the grave.

It does not appear, though every stone and every fragment of a stone has been carefully examined, that any monument or inscription of any kind marked the place where his dust was deposited. "The memorial of his mortality," says Gifford, "is given with a pathetic brevity, which accords but too well with the obscure and humble passages of his life: March 20, 1639-40, buried Philip Massinger, A STRANGER."

Such is all the information that remains to us of this distinguished poet. But though we are ignorant of every circumstance respecting him but that he lived, wrote, and died, we may yet form some idea of his personal character from the recommendatory poems prefixed to his several plays, in which, as Mr. Gifford justly observes, the language of his panegyrists, though warm, expresses an attachment apparently derived not so much from his talents as his virtues: he is their beloved, much-esteemed, dear, worthy, deserving, honoured, long-known, and long-loved friend. All the writers of his life represent him as a man of singular modesty, gentleness, candour, and affability; nor does it appear that he ever made or found an enemy.

FOOTNOTES:

[1] *The register of his birth is not to be found, but all writers of his life agree in naming this city as the place of his nativity; and their account is corroborated by the college entry, which styles him Salisburiensis.*

[2] Dedication to The Bondman.

[3] Singer's edition, p. 120.

[4] Introduction to the Works of Massinger, p. xxxviii.

[5] Vol. ii. p. 933.

[6] Life of Wolsey, p. 517.

[7] The entry in the college book styles him "Phillip Massinger, Salisburiensis, generosi filius."

[8] Dedication to the folio edition of Shakspeare.

[9] Indulgences were granted to those who attended the representation of them.

[10] Gorboduc appeared in 1562; Gammer Gurton, in 1566.

[11] Reed's Shakspeare, vol. iii. p. 83, note 3.

[12] Reed's Shakspeare, vol. iii. p. 15.

[13] Gifford's Massinger, vol. i. p. 103.

[14] This question ought to be set at rest, methinks, by the following extract from the Book of Revels, the oldest that exists, in the office of the auditors of the imprest: "Mrs. Dane, the lynnen dealer, for canvass to paynte for houses for the players, and other properties, as monsters, great hollow trees, and such other, twenty dozen ells, 12l."—See Boswell's Shakspeare, vol. iii. p. 364, et seq.

[15] The first woman who appeared in a regular drama, on a public stage, played Desdemona, about the year 1660. Her name is unknown.

[16] Nat. Field. This celebrated actor played female parts. He was the author of two comedies: A Woman's a Weathercock, 1612, and Amends for Ladies, 1618. He also assisted Massinger in The Fatal Dowry.

[17] Robert Daborne was the author of two plays: The Christian turned Turk, 1612, and The poor Man's Comfort, 1655. He was a gentleman of liberal education, master of arts, and in holy orders. It is supposed that he had preferment in Ireland. A sermon by him, preached at Waterford, in 1618, is extant.

[18] Additions to Malone's Hist. Account of Eng. Stage, p. 488.

As would be expected many works from this time not longer exist either in part or their entirety. Further many playwrights collaborated on plays or revised them for later performances and we have used the latest position known on each of them for the bibliography below..

Solo Plays
The Maid of Honour, tragicomedy (c. 1621; printed 1632)
The Duke of Milan, tragedy (c. 1621–3; printed 1623, 1638)
The Unnatural Combat, tragedy (c. 1621–6; printed 1639)
The Bondman, tragicomedy (licensed 3 December 1623; printed 1624)
The Renegado, tragicomedy (licensed 17 April 1624; printed 1630)
The Parliament of Love, comedy (licensed 3 November 1624; MS)
A New Way to Pay Old Debts, comedy (c. 1625; printed 1632)
The Roman Actor, tragedy (licensed 11 October 1626; printed 1629)
The Great Duke of Florence, tragicomedy (licensed 5 July 1627; printed 1636)
The Picture, tragicomedy (licensed 8 June 1629; printed 1630)
The Emperor of the East, tragicomedy (licensed 11 March 1631; printed 1632)
Believe as You List, tragedy (rejected by the censor in January, but licensed 6 May 1631; MS)
The City Madam, comedy (licensed 25 May 1632; printed 1658)
The Guardian, comedy (licensed 31 October 1633; printed 1655)
The Bashful Lover, tragicomedy (licensed 9 May 1636; printed 1655)

Collaborations with John Fletcher
Sir John van Olden Barnavelt, tragedy (August 1619; MS)
The Little French Lawyer, comedy (c. 1619–23; printed 1647)
A Very Woman, tragicomedy (c. 1619–22; licensed 6 June 1634; printed 1655)
The Custom of the Country, comedy (c. 1619–23; printed 1647)
The Double Marriage, tragedy (c. 1619–23; Printed 1647)
The False One, history (c. 1619–23; printed 1647)
The Prophetess, tragicomedy (licensed 14 May 1622; printed 1647)
The Sea Voyage, comedy (licensed 22 June 1622; printed 1647)
The Spanish Curate, comedy (licensed 24 October 1622; printed 1647)
The Lovers' Progress or The Wandering Lovers, tragicomedy (licensed 6 Dec 1623; rev 1634; printed 1647)
The Elder Brother, comedy (c. 1625; printed 1637).

Collaborations with John Fletcher and Francis Beaumont
Thierry and Theodoret, tragedy (c. 1607?; printed 1621)
The Coxcomb, comedy (1608–10; printed 1647)
Beggars' Bush, comedy (c. 1612–15?; revised 1622?; printed 1647)
Love's Cure, comedy (c. 1612–15?; revised 1625?; printed 1647).

Collaborations with John Fletcher and Nathan Field
The Honest Man's Fortune, tragicomedy (1613; printed 1647)
The Queen of Corinth, tragicomedy (c. 1616–18; printed 1647)
The Knight of Malta, tragicomedy (c. 1619; printed 1647).

Collaborations with Nathan Field
The Fatal Dowry, tragedy (c. 1619, printed 1632); adapted by Nicholas Rowe: The Fair Penitent

Collaborations with John Fletcher, John Ford, and William Rowley, or John Webster
The Fair Maid of the Inn, comedy (licensed 22 January 1626; printed 1647).

Collaborations with John Fletcher, Ben Jonson, and George Chapman

Rollo Duke of Normandy, or The Bloody Brother, tragedy (c. 1616–24; printed 1639).

Collaborations with Thomas Dekker:
The Virgin Martyr, tragedy (licensed 6 October 1620; printed 1622).

Collaborations with Thomas Middleton and William Rowley:
The Old Law, comedy (c. 1615–18; printed 1656).